# BIG NOTES

## How a Stradivarius Makes Money and Music

*by John Axelrod*

*Published by Clink Street Publishing 2021*



*First edition.*



*ISBN:*

*978-1-913962-21-0 - paperback*
*978-1-913962-22-7 - ebook*
*978-1-913962-23-4 - hardback*

# About the author

John Axelrod is the rare breed of conductor who excels at classical and, especially, at pops and crossover repertoire. With an extraordinarily diverse repertoire, innovative programming and charismatic performance style, John Axelrod continues to increase his profile as one of today's leading conductors and is sought after by orchestras and opera houses throughout the world. His persuasive baton technique has been applauded by critics as has his communicative skills with musicians and audiences no matter the culture or language. Presently, Mr. Axelrod is the Principal Conductor of the City of Kyoto Symphony Orchestra and founder of the Concerts Culinaires de Chardonne. Since 2001, Mr. Axelrod has conducted over 175 orchestras around the world, 35 operas and 65 world premieres. Mr. Axelrod has recorded core and contemporary repertoire for Sony Classical, Warner Classics, Ondine, Universal, Naïve and Nimbus.

As an author, Mr. Axelrod has published two books and writes for his own blog. As an educator, Mr. Axelrod has conducted most of the world's professional youth orchestras and regularly teaches via his www.conductorsmasterclassonline.com. As a philanthropist, Mr. Axelrod founded CultureALL

Association which is committed to providing cultural access to underprivileged communities.

Mr. Axelrod graduated in 1988 from Harvard University. At the age of sixteen, John Axelrod was invited to study with Leonard Bernstein; he also studied at the St. Petersburg Conservatory with Ilya Musin in 1996.

"Wie großartige Musik entseht... oder auch nicht".
Bärenreiter/Seeman Henschel Verlag ©2012

Bärenreiter/Seeman Henschel, in August, 2012.
"Griffige Anekdoten und knallige Pointen"
"Striking anecdotes and serious points"
« Der Spiegel », Werner Theurich

*Lenny and Me: On Conducting Bernstein* by John Axelrod, contains analytical commentary about Bernstein's three symphonies and provides publisher information to rent or purchase scores with CD/ DVD/YouTube references.
Amazon Books ©2015

http://iambacchus.com/Beethoven/
Blog about wine and music with over 50,000 viewers

# Including interviews with:

Edward Wulfson, Geneva, Collector, Dealer, Pedagogue

Simon Morris, Director, J & A Beare Auction House, London

Christopher Marinello, Art Recovery International

Florian Leonhard, Luthier, Collector

Tamio Kano, Managing Director,
The Nippon Music Foundation

Frank Almond, Concertmaster Milwaukee Symphony

Suzanne Fushi, President, Stradivari Society

Virginia Villa, Director General, Museo del Violino, Cremona

Jonathan Moulds CBE, Collector, Board Member
London Symphony Orchestra

Nigel Brown OBE, Stradivari Trust

Jason Price, Tarisio Auction House

Bruno Price and Ziv Arazi, Rare Violins of New York/
In Consortium

In the 1998 movie *The Red Violin*, a great violin maker named Nicolo Bussotti, based on the real-life luthier Antonio Stradivari, supposedly mixes the blood of his deceased beloved wife into the varnish of what is to be his most precious creation. The violin's journey, from its creation in Cremona in 1681 until its auction in 1997, with all the places and persons that possessed it in between, is the story of the film. It is a story about music, memories and money.

The violin somehow survives all odds – despite being smuggled, being hit by storms, being stolen, shipped, and even being sweat upon by a Paganini-like soloist – and the red varnish remains pure and potent in its appeal. So much so that the expert appraiser himself, recognising its provenance and potential, manages to switch a perfect copy at the moment of the auction, only to disappear, thus continuing the unlikely story of this red violin. Everyone wanted it. Yet, none could possess it forever. The violin, as music itself, exists out of time for all time. The violin, itself made of wood, is finite. Its value is priceless. Its sound is immortal.

Is it possible to purchase immortality? Imagine really buying this fictitious fiddle. How much would it cost? During the auction in the final scene of the film, the figures surpass $2 million. In real life, the *Red Mendelssohn* – the Stradivarius of 1720 on which *The Red Violin* is based – sold for $1.7 million in 1990 and is now owned by the violinist Elizabeth Pitcairn. Over the next twenty years, the value of this Stradivarius, and all other rare violins, violas and cellos, has increased exponentially. Today, it could be worth over $16 million.

In 2012, J & A Beare in London set the world record for the most expensive violin privately sold with the 1741 *Vieuxtemps* Guarneri del Gesù for over $16 million. Its new owner anonymously donated the historic instrument to the violinist Anne Akiko Meyers, on loan for the rest of her life. The violin is said to be in remarkably fine condition, with very little corrective work or restoration. The name was bestowed upon the violin after being owned by the Belgian nineteenth century violinist Henri Vieuxtemps and was later played by Yehudi Menuhin and Pinchas Zukerman, among others.

Public auctions have also set record sales. In 2011, an anonymous bidder at the Tarisio Auction House paid £9,808,000 ($15,894,000 or 11,076,000 euros) for the 1721 *Lady Blunt* Stradivarius, named after Lord Byron's granddaughter Lady Anne Blunt, who owned it for thirty years. The price was over four times the previous auction record for a Stradivarius violin. That is one expensive lady.

Is $16 million for a violin too much to pay? Not these days, especially when they can be reauctioned for twice the price. According to the Stradivari Society, in an article published in 2008, rare violins that have been sold for millions have never decreased in value and from 1960–2008 have consistently outperformed both the Dow Jones Industrial Average (DJIA) and precious metals by an enormous percentage: a 19,400% increase for the violins versus up to 1800% for precious metals and DJIA.

**Market Analysis: Appreciation of Stradivari and Guarneri *del Gesù* Violins, Silver, Gold, and Platinum Prices and the Dow Jones Industrial Average (DJIA), 1960–2008[1]**

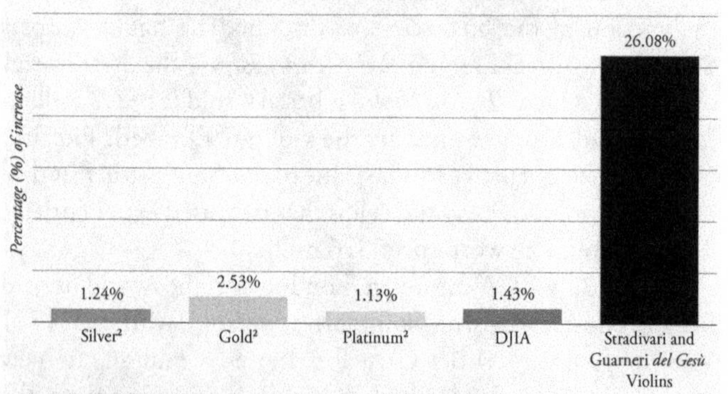


1 Precious metal and DJIA values on the last trading day of the year.
2 Price per ounce.
3 1960–2005: annual average price of Stradivari and Guarneri *del Gesù* Violjns. 2006–2008 values are based on the retail sale prices of twenty-seven Stradivari and Guameri *del Gesù* violins sold during that period. The average price typically reflects many more low-end sales than record sales since top examples come on the market infrequently. The sale prices in this group range from $1.24 to $10.5 million.

**Comparison: Stradivari and Guarneri *del Gesù* Violin Prices and the Dow Jones Lndustrial Average (DJIA), Percentage of Increase, 1960–2008**

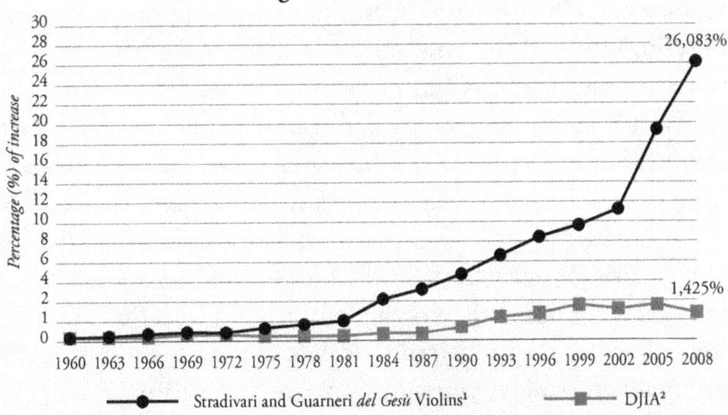


1 1960–2005: annual average price of Stradivari and Guameri *del Gesù* Violins. 2006–2008 values are based on the retail sale prices of twenty-seven Stradivari and Guarneri *del Gesù* violins sold during that period. The average price typically reflects many more low-end sales than record sales since top examples come on the market infrequently. The sale prices in this group range from $1.24 to $10.5 million.

2 DJIA values on the last trading day of the year.

**Comparison: Stradivari and Guarneri *del Gesù* Violin and Gold Prices, Percentage of Increase 1960–2008**

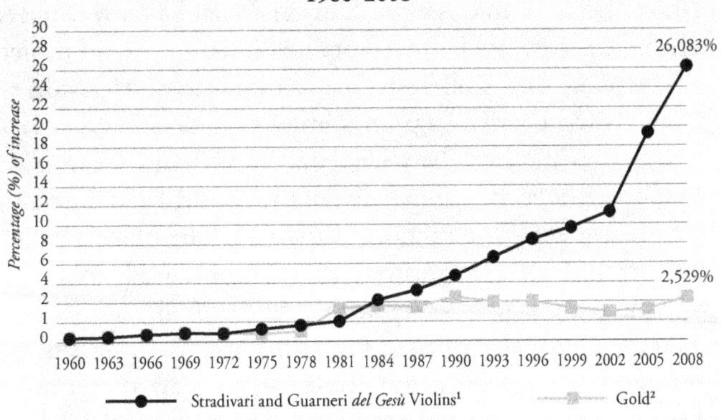


1 1960–2005: annual average price of Stradivari and Guameri *del Gesù* Violins. 2006–2008 values are based on the retail sale prices of twenty-seven Stradivari and Guarneri *del Gesù* violins sold during that period. The average price typically reflects many more low-end sales than record sales since top examples come on the market infrequently. The sale prices in this group range from $1.24 to $10.5 million.

2 Price per ounce. Gold values as of the last trading day of the year.

By 2021 standards, their appreciation in value has seen exponential gains yet to be estimated. In other words, rare violins are a benchmark of profitability, requiring big bank notes to buy, and the Stradivarius is at the top of the chart for most serious collectors and investors.

Whatever the motivations, all these people who pay for a Stradivarius or any other rare instrument (or steal or copy one) have in common one very important thing: they are investing in immortality. Not in the sense of living forever in a futuristic fantasy like cryogenics, or in the idea of housing a piece of art in perpetuity, but in their own identification with the immortal itself. Even if they outwardly declare being only a custodian, internally they all are consciously aware such an investment can carry their own name into the books of cultural history.

People who steal them may have the same motivation to have their names live beyond their lifetime, but mostly they just want the money. Thus, the business of beating death by becoming a modern-day Medici (or even a Vincenzo Peruggia, who famously stole the *Mona Lisa*) is booming. And it is not only a good return on investment, especially now when stock markets are as volatile as a rollercoaster. What better way to get rich and write yourself into history books than to be the owner, or the *voleur*, of a violin once played by Yehudi Menuhin or Jascha Heifetz or even Paganini himself?

The relationship between the artist and patron is symbiotic. The relationship between the criminal and the buyer is co-dependent. One cannot exist without the other. History has shown how the greatest art ever produced coincided with the patronage of enlightened, culturally literate leaders, whether noble, papal or civic. Other than acts of terrorism, the greatest crimes against culture have often occurred as a result of such patronage. It need not be the criminal mind these days. Now, as governments around the globe cut culture in the face of austerity measures or budget deficits, coronavirus pandemics and stimulus packages, and corporations focus more on their bottom line and shareholder value, individuals and their foundations have begun to fill the philanthropic gap, finding ways to not only support good causes on humanitarian levels and participate in the creation and conservation of culture, but to also satisfy that very same urge that inspired those patrons of yesterday to protect their future name. Sometimes that name is preserved simply by the assets in the attic or the art museum. Other times the name is associated with the asset in the arms of a great artist. And if it is a Stradivarius, that asset only appreciates in both value and reputation.

To be deemed a true Stradivarius, an instrument must come from the workshop of the Stradivari family during the seventeenth and eighteenth centuries. The patriarch of that family, Antonio Stradivari, made approximately 1000 string instruments of which only an estimated 650 still exist. Most are in the multimillion-dollar range and can only increase in value. It can be even said that a "Strad" is worth more than its weight in gold. It has been compared to the voice of God. One cannot easily put a price tag on that.

## What is a "Strad?"

A "Strad" is the nickname given to a string instrument made by Antonio Stradivari. According to Toby Faber, author of *Stradivari's Genius: Five Violins, One Cello and Three Centuries of Enduring Perfection*, these instruments are more than mere fiddles made by Antonio Stradivari. A Strad is the stuff of legend, the X on the musical map of treasures and, in some cases, considered the equivalent of the second coming. The *Messiah*, finished in 1716, is considered by Faber to be "the most famous violin in the world." It is worth knowing a bit of this history of the *Messiah* which itself could be a movie plot competitive with *The Red Violin*. It may inspire many an investor to seek and find the coming of the new Messiah.

*The Messiah Stradivarius, courtesy of the Ashmolean Museum, Oxford, England.*

The *Messiah* is said to sound "like hearing the angels sing." Even if it is classified as a "Golden Period" violin, that is made between 1700 and 1725, it looks as if it was just made by the master himself. There are literally no cracks or scratches, no defects or holes. Even the varnish remains completely intact. A major fact is the instrument has almost never been played as only a few violinists have ever been allowed to hold it. It is also rumoured that Stradivari decided that this violin was the only one of his instruments that was not for sale. His sons, Francesco and Omobono, retained the *Messiah* for their lives. In 1775, Stradivari's youngest son, Paolo, sold it to the art collector Count Cozio di Salabue. Eventually, in 1827, the violin was in the possession of the famous Italian instrument dealer Luigi Tarisio (from where the auction house gets its name). And yet, despite his self-promotion as the owner of the *Messiah*, he kept it hidden. That explains why the French violin virtuoso Delphin Alard remarked to Tarisio: "Your violin is like the Messiah; one always expects him, but he never appears." The name stuck and became legend.

After Tarisio's death in 1885, the French violin maker Jean-Baptiste Vuillaume found the violin hidden in an attic. Himself a master luthier, Vuillaume made about twenty-five copies of the violin and kept it for the remainder of his life, declaring the violin "the wonder of wonders." In 1939, the Hill Brothers in London inherited the *Messiah*, and bequeathed it to the Ashmolean Museum in Oxford on the strict condition that it not be played.

Imagine then the astounding shock when in 1998, the instrument was tested for its origin, provenance, handcraft and documentation, and the result of this carbon testing suggested that the wood had only been carved after the death of Stradivari himself and that the violin could therefore not have been a work of the master craftsman. The scandal reverberated through centuries. The Ashmolean authorities had no choice but to demand a retraction. Out of necessity another test reconfirmed the violin's authenticity. And yet, doubt remains. If it is real, it is the most valuable Stradivarius still in known existence. If it is a forgery, then, of course, the question is the same as posed in the movie *The Red Violin* (and mindfully the same question asked among all Christians): Wherefore art thou, O Messiah?

The wood is an important consideration. The master luthier Florian Leonhard, himself an apprentice to the Hill Brothers, was interviewed about the making of the *Messiah* and if he, like Vuillaume, could recreate the genius of this instrument:

> In many years of making violins and ingesting information, I can start from different angles; From the makers point of view. Can it be recreated? On a large scale to recreate a Strad, no. Unlike politicians who like to mumble, I like to say no. I believe if somebody is an expert analyzer of these original rare instruments, and see hundreds by the maker, not only in photographs and

museums but hold them and understand with hands, restoring them then it cannot be excluded that this person has access to so much information about this maker that he can if he has the skills it is possible to recreate the instrument. You can understand because I worked with the best shops in the world – like Hill & Sons – I saw so many Strads so I knew what was the best. You didn't waste time to guess what was the best. You could trust the opinion of Hill. I could learn the language. Why did he create the best? Why was I so far away from it as a maker? It took me 25 years of my career to the wood. I think the sources are not wrong about Venice seawater wood. Ice age wood is what he used for 1690s. He went away from the ice age. It doesn't mean they are not amazing, long violins are great, but the Golden Period used Venetian wood.

So on a small scale, a few people like me, who held, restored, played, dealt, I call them TRUE COPIES – I'm not making a copy. It's like the soul of the violin. Not pretending I am better than Stradivari. I am looking up at Stradivari. He created something we embraced worldwide as an iconic thing; by any genius today will never be surpassed; No matter how many I make that sound just as good, I have fooled people. I put five Strad and my violin in the middle and 60% of the time the players choose mine. Like a wine maker, if you grow up early with wine you can recreate like the best.

If you make the test, two of those winning violins came from me. Only the leading violin makers in the world were able to offer. So the best offered the best. The full truth is the handful of great violins are only possible to be heard.

The varnish is always there. The ground is there and that makes the wood vibrate the way it does. When I make a violin now to make a Strad quality that lasts even if mine are equally famous; Mine in the end is a copy. An investor

> would choose the original over the new. I am a craftsman with an artistic angle. I'm not an artist, like Stradivari.
>
> There are people who order from me for that reason. Because they believe in the future of the name of this violin. I had a 100% increase in the value of the violin. I only started this eight years ago. When I became a violin maker it was just a dream. I kept my violins from sale. Only now when I feel I am wiser.
>
> Yes, it is possible in a limited way to copy a Strad. Some people could master it. Will it affect Stradivarius value? Because Stradivari is always a finite number, and so expensive some cannot afford, but the demand will always be high.

Jason Price, the founder and director of the Tarisio Auction House, provides more perspective on rare versus new instruments:

> Some argue that modern instruments can sound just as good as the old masters but for me this comparison is irrelevant and misses the point.
>
> Scholars and collectors of paintings don't compare Rembrandt to Warhol – how could they? It's a question of apples and oranges. And for me the same is true for new versus old violins: they each have merits and should be appreciated differently, not ranked on a linear scale of better and worse.

Bruno Price and Ziv Arazi of In Consortium believe the Italian rare instruments are singular and unique, despite the advances of modern instruments. They require maximum talent to bring out the potential.

> It is not possible to replicate one of the great old instruments. Makers have tried for almost 200 years but

to the player the difference is immediately obvious. If you spent hours in a Formula 1 car simulator you might have the potential to become a competent driver. But if you were then placed in a real F1 car the chances of being able to maximize its performance is very slight. A top professional driver can do it, and when pushing himself to the absolute limit with countless reactions in 100ths of seconds, the genius and artistry becomes evident. And like the top violinist, the great drivers are happiest when they are challenged and pushed to be better.

Jonathan Moulds CBE is considered by many to be the most sophisticated rare instrument collector and investor today. Despite the results of this blind hearing, Jonathan Moulds is also convinced the rare instrument is better. The rare instruments used may not have been among the best quality, or the players may have been too timid to express themselves on the antique as they would on the modern. Holding $16 million in the hands does have an impact on the psychology and physiology of a player.

In defence of his opinion, Moulds says:

I suspect modern instruments and therefore modern makers are accomplished. Historically, there were only a number of makers, but limited to a small number of families. Guarneri, Stradivari, Amati, but among modern instruments there are many good ones. I thought about that. I've heard modern instruments played. Powerhouses of sound, but not the nuance and complexity. Same can be said about wine. New World wines are powerhouses that last five years. Bordeaux last decades and brings different colours and perspectives. The modern wine can be powerful and good to drink. You know, I participated in a blind hearing test, two of them over ten years, in fact. I listened and even provided some instruments,

> three or four for each one. But even if the person playing was considered among the top 25 best soloists, they are still quite timid with it. Consequences of damaging it and it being so expensive, so I don't get the best out of the instrument. Like a Ferrari. Trying to compare things that are rarefied depends on the people involved with the testing. If you and I drove eight Formula 1 cars around the track we would not know anything about the car, only the driver. Marginal things, but history shows, when professionals do it and are not worried about value but about performance, then you can tell. Ive seen them play with timidity. Have to get used to an instrument. These blind tests have an agenda. Having heard modern and old instruments played spectacularly well, there is an art to getting the best tone from the instrument. In terms of the colors you can hear in the best concert halls, the Italians are the best.

David Fulton, the esteemed collector, agrees with the need to master the instruments. He says about the violins he has sold:

> These are virtuoso tools. For me to play the *General Kyd* Stradivarius (1714) or the *Carrodus* Guarnerius del Gesù (1743) is like trying to drive a Ferrari in traffic. You don't play Mozart quartets with them. When the soloist Vadim Repin played the *Carrodus* in concert he said it was "like trying to ride a wild horse."

The *Messiah* is not alone in esteem and value. The gospel of Stradivari has spread far and wide. The *Viotti ex-Bruce*, finished in 1709, is, according to Faber, "a perfect Stradivarius in every respect." Named after the brilliant virtuoso Giovanni Battista Viotti, the violin was offered to the Royal Academy of Music in 2002 in lieu of inheritance tax by the son of its previous owner, John Bruce, with a market value of £3.5 million. The *Prince Khevenhüller* of 1733 is named for Prince

Johann Sigismund Friedrich de Khevenhüller-Metsch, who purchased it as a gift for his second wife. With a provenance that has been proven relevant with many different owners, it was valued at over $4 million and today could be worth twice as much. A quartet of Stradivarius instruments — two violins, a viola and a cello — have a cult history to their name. The legendary Italian violinist and composer, Niccolo Paganini (the quartet's namesake) acquired each of the instruments individually in the early 19th century. Each had its own personal name:
1st Violin: *Comte Cozio di Salabue* (1727)
2nd Violin: *Desaint* (1680, Stradivari's early Amatise style)
Viola: *Mendelssohn* (1731, one of less than twelve surviving Strad violas)
Cello: *Ladenburg* (1736)

Following Paganini, the quartet was divided and frequently changed owners before being united again by Emil Herrmann, a prominent New York dealer and restorer. The instruments were purchased by Anna E. Clark for the formation of a new quartet in 1946 — thus began the "Paganini Quartet." After the quartet disbanded, the instruments were played by the Cleveland String Quartet until the Nippon Music Foundation bought the instruments in 1994 and loaned them to the Tokyo String Quartet until 2013, then the Hagen Quartet, and are presently loaned to the Quartetto di Cremona. The value has not been disclosed. The amount can only be imagined.

The 1711 *Duport* Stradivarius cello, considered the most expensive cello in the world, was purchased by the Nippon Foundation for $20 million. This instrument has a pedigree worthy of its elevated price. In 1812 Jean-Louis Duport, then the cello's owner, was in Paris, where he met Napoleon Bonaparte. The cello to this day bears a dent that was supposedly made by Napoleon's boot when the emperor unsuccessfully attempted to play the instrument. Mstislav Rostropovich played the instrument from 1974 till his death in 2007.

The *Davidov* is another Stradivarius cello, finished in 1712. Once played by Jacqueline du Pré, and now owned by the company Moët Hennessy Louis Vuitton, it was given to the legendary cellist Yo-Yo Ma to play "for life." He also plays a cello made in 1733 by Domenico Montagnana, oddly named *Petunia*, its name given by one of Ma's students.

And, then comes the *Lipinski*. Named after the eighteenth-century virtuoso Karol Lipinski, this violin was made in 1715, and is the ideal vintage, as this considered the epicentre of Stradivari's Golden Period. The *Lipinski*, has more than provenance. It has a plot that could be worthy of a Netflix crime story. Why? Is it easy to become a millionaire by stealing a Strad? How hard is it to sell a Strad? As a patron, how can you tell the difference between the merely good and the truly great? As a thief, how can you know whether you have a Stradivarius or not? Immortality is both a blessing and an expression of liberty. For better or worse, some names are immortal just because of the story surrounding their sinister plots.

In 2014, the concertmaster of the Milwaukee Symphony Orchestra, Frank Almond, was leaving a concert with the 1715 *Lipinski* Strad. A thief who had been monitoring Almond's every move for weeks, approached him with a taser and stole the violin, worth $6 million at the time.

"There was an automatic assumption the violin would be traveling interstate and then most likely overseas," said Special Agent Dave Bass, a member of the Art Crime Team in the Bureau's Milwaukee Division.

Special Agents Tim Bisswurm and Brian Due began gathering information about the weapon used in the robbery, which break open the case. Using evidence found at the crime scene, agents were able in a few days to trace the weapon from the manufacturer to the purchaser – a Milwaukee barber named, and I do not kid, "Universal Knowledge Allah". Somehow this name even tops that of *Figaro*, though I doubt the UKA opera is in the works, but one never knows.

Frank Almond said during our interview:

> I knew what was happening after I was tazed, but what I initially thought was the guy was taking my picture. So I came out after a reception and he pulled in next to me in the parking lot. A beat-up van, still running. Like a Scooby Doo Van. It was a clue for the authorities, but I didn't think of it at the time. Turns out he planned this for two or three years.
>
> Here's the thing. It becomes worthless when they steal it. It didn't occur to these guys. As far as I know and others know, this is the only case on record when one person specifically targeted a high-end instrument, a specific one, and tried to steal it.

Worthless because it would have been easily discovered if the thief had tried to openly sell the Strad. Covertly sold is another matter. If it was stolen to be given to a buyer who would keep it under lock and key, it might have never been heard or seen again. The case of the 1713 *Gibson ex-Huberman* Strad is just like that. In 1936, A young violinist named Julian Altman, took Huberman's violin and case from his dressing room while Huberman gave a recital in Carnegie Hall. The violin was never recovered while Huberman lived. Only before Altman's death fifty years later was it revealed to his wife that he kept the violin to play, covering it with shoe polish to hide the original red varnish. The violin was sold in 1988 to the British violinist Norbert Brainin, and then eventually purchased by the soloist Joshua Bell for under $4 million.

The *Lipinski* was not stolen by a violinist. Instead, by a career criminal named Salah Salahaydn. When a $100,000 reward was announced, police received a tip regarding Salahaydn. A week after the robbery, UKA and Salahaydn were arrested and charged. It turns out Salahaydn never even had the intention to sell the instrument. He stole it for reward money. Not a bad idea, except that he was arrested years earlier for doing the same thing with a sculpture.

### *The Dimwit Factor*

Many Stradivarius violins, like the one stolen in Milwaukee, are valued so high not just for their age and craftsmanship but also for their impressive line of owners. Being stolen made it even more notorious. The *Lipinski* became so famous the violin even has its own Wikipedia page. Almond spoke about the aftermath:

> When the *Lipinski* came back we were terrified that it wouldn't be looked after and damaged. Part of the plea-bargain to not be put away for a longer sentence was Salahadyn had to return it in good condition, not as kindling or damaged. It turned out, for the most part, it wasn't damaged at all.
>
> Amazing to me, even though he put it in a suitcase found in an attic of a house on the southside of Milwaukee.
>
> (Yes, again an attic. Remember the *Messiah*?)
>
> When the FBI and police showed up, it was 30 degrees Fahrenheit in the house, kept like a bottle of wine. Yeah, it had a few bumps and bruises, like scratches; but I remember playing it a few days later and it sounded great. Bows were also nicked up. But here was the Dimwit Factor. The guy's driver's license was in the suitcase with the violin. That captured these mastermind criminals. Real smart guys.

The *Lipinski* and the *Gibson* are not the only famous Strads having been snatched or misplaced. Stories abound of dimwits on and off stage. In 2010, a thief stole a 1696 Strad worth nearly $2 million from the violinist Min-Jin Kym in a branch of Prêt-a-Manger near Euston station in London. The thief had no idea what he had stolen and tried to sell it to the bus driver for £100. Her Peccatte bow itself was worth $100,000. Lark Insurance Broking Group paid out the claim and, fortunately, it was recovered by British detectives in Bulgaria two years later.

In 2009, the former New York Philharmonic concertmaster Glenn Dicterow left a 1727 Guarneri del Gesù violin in a taxi while on his way to Carnegie Hall. The driver realised to whom the violin belonged. He hurried back to the concert hall just in time to give Dicterow his instrument. How do you get to Carnegie Hall? Practice, pay your taxi and please don't forget your instrument.

The soloist Philippe Quint left his $4 million 1708 *Ruby* Stradivarius, on loan from the Stradivari Society, in a Newark, N.J., taxi cab after a flight home from Dallas. The cab driver, Mohammed Khalil, returned the violin within hours and Quint played a special private concert for the Newark Taxi Cab Association to show his gratitude. He also gave Mr. Khalil a $100 tip for the safe return of the instrument. And Khalil got a medal from the city. Cabbies can be so crucial in times of crisis.

How does all this happen? The Dimwit Factor.

I myself recall a time in Paris while having dinner at the home of some friends when the violinist Ivry Gitlis, who was discussing the sale of his 1713 *Sancy* Stradivarius suddenly realized he forgot his cell phone in the back of the taxi on the way to their home. Thankfully, it was not the violin. But given his hysteria to recover his phone, he seemed to treat it equally to his Strad. After the taxi service had been contacted and the taxi traced, the driver, also named Mohammed, returned the phone, while Ivry anxiously waited. Ivry was an Israeli. Mohammed came from Egypt. At that moment, when Ivry thanked him profusely and kissed his hands, Middle East peace was solved. Ivry passed away on Christmas Eve, 2020, at ninety-eight years old, and I might add that despite this momentary respite between old tribes, Middle East peace has actually not happened, and, like the sale of the *Messiah* Strad, may never come to pass.

Not all Stradivarius violins make it back to their rightful owners, though. According to the FBI, in 1994, a Stradivarius from 1727, forever known as the *Davidoff-Morini*, was worth $4 million dollars at the time it was stolen from a dying violinist's apartment. The theft is a story made for Sherlock Holmes. A certain Erika Morini, a child prodigy who had a substantially long career as a soloist, died at the age of ninety-one of heart failure. She had been in New York's Mount Sinai Hospital and had no idea that her valuable violin along with paintings, letters and scores had been stolen from her apartment. Despite the *Davidoff-Morini* violin sitting on the FBI's top ten art crimes list, there has been no information about the violin leading to any recovery. There is some speculation that because Erika's fingering notes and music were stolen the thief might have been a violinist, or that the theft was carried out as a crime for hire for another violinist. Today it would be worth over $10 million, but it has yet to be found.

Sometimes, the Stradivarius is lost not by being stolen. The Dimwit Factor rears its ugly head when the soloist fails to care for the priceless antiquity that it is. In 2008, the crossover violinist, David Garrett, affectionately known as the "David Beckham of the violin" for his good looks and long blond hair, accidentally tripped coming down the stairs from the Barbican stage and stepped on his Stradivarius *San Lorenzo*, irreparably damaging the violin, causing over £60,000 in restoration and risking its immortal sound would become suddenly and irreversibly mortal. His father was a dealer so it might be imagined he would know how to take better care. The replacement 1718 Stradivarius, arranged by Beare and flown in from Milano, required a three-man security crew to monitor his every move. The audience could watch Mr. Garrett. The security guards watched the violin. Garrett was flummoxed:

> People said it was as if I'd trodden on a banana skin. I fell down a flight of steps and onto the case. When I opened it, the violin was in pieces. I couldn't speak and I couldn't get up. I didn't even know if I was hurt – I didn't care. I'd had that violin for eight years. It was like losing a friend.

Even genius artists can be affected by that Dimwit Factor. Remember that 1733 Montagnana cello named *Petunia* and played by Yo-Yo Ma? In 1999, he left it in the trunk of a New York taxi. It became international headline news. A huge crowd gathered outside his hotel the next day to see it returned in a black police sedan. Who died? Montagnana might have had another case of the "hypochondria" which was reportedly his cause of death in Venice in 1750. Imagine Stradivari himself rolling around in his grave had he known about all these Dimwit episodes.

Then again, Antonio Stradivari might have foreseen the spectacle and sensation surrounding his creations and perhaps would have relished all the attention. He was a meticulous marketer, providing the supply to meet the demands of the many patrons, noble, papal, and otherwise wealthy who wanted his work, including the Medici, who ordered these precious instruments by the dozens. The love affair with violins started before Stradivari, when Catherine de Medici in the mid-sixteenth century, exiled to France for an arranged marriage, ordered a set of thirty-eight stringed instruments from Cremona. The workshop of Andrea Amati and his family became synonymous with craftsmanship and quality, gaining respectability for the violin and earning a royal reward. With Catherine's patronage, the violin became popular among the elite, and the stage was set for the great age of Cremonese luthiers. The Medici family continued this illustrious legacy of cultivating creative geniuses and Antonio Stradivari was the beneficiary of this bounty. The Medici were not only bankers and investors. The family business of their cultural patronage led to the commissioning of five of Stradivari's most beautiful instruments: the "Medici Quintet," which today includes the *Medici* Stradivarius of 1716, one of the most outstanding of his creations. Stradivari had many customers who valued his instruments as much as they treasured their estates, conquests and other assets. Amati was the grandfather and master craftsman. With Stradivari, the term genius was applied. And his was a remarkable life, living until he was ninety-three, astonishing for a man of the 1700s. He kept his manuals intact, tutoring not only his own children but transforming the tradition of Cremonese luthiers for centuries to come. The instruments, like the man, may be mortal, but as we have come to understand, the name lives forever.

## *Just who was Stradivari?*

The name of Antonio Stradivari – Stradivarius, in the familiar Latinised form of his name – is not unlike that of Leonardo da Vinci, in being considered universally as an artistic superlative of genius, representative of a pinnacle of craftsmanship achieved three centuries ago in Cremona, Italy. A Leonardo painting is rare in supply but is only a painting. It is sublime and produces an intangible impact in the viewer. But it is a concrete canvas covered in oil and human gesture. The violin is also a concrete piece of carved wood, strung and hollowed. But it is not only an instrument but also an unreproducible original piece of abstract sound. That very sound transcends boundaries, descriptions and time itself. It is the marriage of the tangible and intangible in ways no other piece of art or antiquity can match.

There are many collectors and dealers who find it a more fitting analogy to compare a Stradivarius to a Formula 1 race car. Both are absolute triumphs of technology that are usually made available only to the talented few who are best qualified to make use of them only through the investment and endowment of a patron. Indeed, as we will discover, most of the celebrated string players in the world, from past to present, play instruments owned by someone else, with both player and owner profiting from this profile and partnership. As noted earlier, Yo-Yo Ma plays the *Davidov* cello, one of several Stradivari instruments owned by the Louis Vuitton Foundation.

The grandfather of the Cremonese school was Andrea Amati, who, with his sons, established the business of being a luthier from the sixteenth to early seventeenth centuries. He added a fourth string to the violin and standardised the size and shapes of the principal string instruments. Stradivari began making violins after his parents sent him to apprentice for Nicolo Amati, Andrea's grandson. Stradivari was twelve years old. Giuseppe Guarneri del Gesù, a contemporary of Stradivari's, whose output was perhaps less in number, but no less in value or expertise, completes the triumvirate.

Early in his development, during the 1680s, Stradivari moved away from Amati's technique and began experimenting with his own style of sound – hole shapes, softer varnish, wider purfling (the inlaid border near the edges of the violin's back and front) and a stronger tone. During the 1690s, there was a distinct identity to his style which made his reputation. Stradivari began crafting what are known as his "Long Strads," employing a darker, richer varnish. By 1698, he discovered what became his unique selling point. It was a shortened instrument, commonly referred to as the "Grand Pattern," which he refined and revised from 1700 through the 1720s, to create the violins during a period now known as Stradivarius' Golden Period. From 1730 until his death, Stradivari was an unconscious master of the trade, whose genius could not be replicated by even those who studied under his tutelage. Even his own children, eleven of them, could not carry on his school, limited as they were to only mortal means. That singular exceptional quality of Stradivari's genius has become the criteria for his incomparable value and the reason why his name is as known today and reserved in the same league of da Vinci, Einstein and Shakespeare.

How did Stradivari make the best? Why was his product above all others? Some say it was the wood. As a successful luthier and businessman, he had access to the best material on the market. Paganini is supposed to have said that Stradivari "only used the wood on trees on which nightingales sang." Stradivari's Golden Period was noted for his particularly excellent wood and other materials. It is also rumoured that Stradivari's wood may have been soaked in seawater because he was able to receive the rejected wood from the Venetian Naval shipbuilders. Varnish was also a mysterious formula. Some say the secret formula of Pozzolana earth, a kind of volcanic ash found in the Cremona region, that might have been applied between the wood and the varnish, gave a more sensitive resonance to the wood fibres of his violins. Others say it was the dry Cremonese air that did the trick. Or it might have been blood. Whatever the reason, Stradivari found his stride, and had copyrights been in effect at that time, his instruments would be worth even far more than they are today.

The common exalting of Stradivari and other old violins over modern instruments is regularly brought into question. In a 2017 article by Claudia Fritz, Joseph Curtin, Jacques Poitevineau and Fan-Chia Tao, published by the *Proceedings of the National Academy of Sciences*, violinists themselves could not tell whether they were playing on a Stradivarius or on a modern violin when the identity of the instrument was unknown. Stradivari dealers tend to dismiss such findings, suggesting that the resources of a great instrument cannot be revealed under testing conditions, especially from the player on stage as the hallmark of these Cremonese masterpieces are their ability to project to a great distance.

"A Stradivari has the ability to deliver the whole range of tonal colours to the back of a big concert hall," Simon Morris, the co-managing director of Beare explained in our interview:

> The perfection of craftsmanship and varnish was also unsurpassed with an extraordinarily large output. Guarneri's and Stradivari's violins have worn over the years to reveal great beauty in the layers of tones and colors in the varnish as well as the sound. The beauty of these instruments can be seen and heard with little understanding of the history – just as with a Mozart symphony. Virtually all contemporary makers today copy one of these two makers. But new violins don't have the range of tonal colour. The depth of personality isn't there.

While the 650 or so Strads that survive are prized by musicians – in part because having access to one is a mark of status that helps secure engagements and media – the sound that a stringed instrument makes is among the least important determinations of its market value. Dealers and auction houses price instruments according to their visible condition, their state of preservation and the desirability of their dimensions. They are after all, pieces of antiquity and cultural treasures, with which modern instruments cannot compete.

## *What makes a Strad so valuable?*

There are only an estimated 650 known Stradivari in the world. And fewer del Gesù. More available and less expensive but no less in demand are violins from Amati, Bergonzi, Guadagnini. Simply put, the limited supply and constant demand stretches the boundaries of valuation. The historical provenance and national cultural identity also increase the estimated value. If a major violinist holds it in his or her hands, the identification and association with that star quality only adds more 0s and commas to the price. Norman Lebrecht, who has published several books about classical music, wrote on his blog *Scena*:

> There are so few Cremona violins in existence to begin with, and the best ones are incredibly prized, and the violins acquire a pedigree that arises from their owners. So a Heifetz Stradivarius or a Perlman Stradivarius automatically increases in value by a six-figure amount.

Strads that have been retouched with a new varnish are considered inferior in value. A non-original scroll (the head of the violin) is another deduction. Necks are another matter without demerits because many necks on rare instruments were altered or changed as composers from the late 1800s composed music that demanded longer fingerboards than Stradivari would have predicted. But there are those rare examples of a Strad whose neck has been preserved. Remember that expensive Lady? As the actress Nia Vardalos is known to have said: "The man may be the head of the household. But the woman is the neck, and she can turn the head whichever way she pleases." No wonder the *Lady Blunt* is the most expensive violin ever purchased at auction. If sold today, that $16 million would be worth at least $18–20 million with a minimum 10% return, even during a coronavirus crisis, and, especially, during the volatility of normal equity investments.

Why does the violin make such a significant return on investment? And what must one know before making such an investment? All this leads, of course, to the inevitable question: How much does a rare instrument cost?

Based on a FranceMusique listing in a 2017 survey by Guillaume Decalf, here is an edited opportunity to view the most expensive rare violins sold at auction with their sale valuations, including previous owners and players for reasons of provenance. Of course, all these instruments have increased in value since then, and a few more have been sold to join this list. The list only gets longer, and the numbers keep going up. There is no buy low, sell high principle. If the violin comes on the market, and you can afford it, buy it above market price because it will only increase and will always remain in demand.

Ladies and Gentleman, here are the top seven most valuable rare violins recently sold at auction, from a perfect Guadagnini to the ideal del Gesù to, of course, the most stunning of Stradivarius *(photos courtesy of Tarisio Auction House)*:

—— 7 ——

The Dorothy Delay Guadagnini - €1 million

An extraordinary violin crafted in 1778 by the Italian luthier Giovanni Battista Guadagnini (1711–1786). The violin is named after its owner Dorothy Delay, arguably the greatest American violinist and teacher. She was an assistant to Ivan Galamian at the Julliard School of Music, where Itzhak Perlman was studying at the time. In her own studio, she taught a Who's Who of great soloists: Albert Stern, Nigel Kennedy, Gil Shaham, Midori, Cho-Liang Lin, Shlomo Mintz and Sarah Chang are among the many. It was auctioned for €1 million at Tarisio in 2013, the highest officially recorded sum for a Guadagnini at that time.

## 6
## The Red Mendelssohn Stradivarius - €1.7 million

*photo courtesy of Elizabeth Pitcairn*

As mentioned at the beginning of the chapter, the *Red Mendelssohn* sale in 1990 for £902,000 was record breaking.

Created in 1720, it was called *The Red Violin* (inspiring the film, The Red Violin) because of its vivid red varnish. The legendary violinist muse and confidant of Brahms and Schumann, Joseph Joachim owned and played the violin, which then disappeared for 100 years before being discovered in Berlin in the 1930s in the ownership of Lili von Mendelssohn (a descendant of Felix Mendelssohn). The heir of a wealthy American industrial family, the Pitcairns, acquired it in 1990. The violin was given to his then only sixteen-year-old granddaughter, Elizabeth Pitcairn, who continues to play it to this day. Elizabeth shared her thoughts about this extraordinary instrument:

> Anyone fortunate enough to have played even a few notes on a Stradivari instrument will remark on the "squillo" - that mystifying operatic trumpet-like voice characteristic which sets these Cremonese instruments apart.
>
> In my 31 year partnership with the 1720 *Red Mendelssohn* Stradivarius, (a fraction of its auspicious 301 years of existence), it is magical with every single performance to experience its unique voice which allows the most delicate pianissimo notes to carry with ultimate clarity and purity to the ears of the listener in the last row of the highest balcony of the largest concert halls of the world.

## 5

## The Folinari Guarnerius Del Gesù - €1.8 million

One of the rare violins made by Giuseppe Antonio Guarneri (1688–1744), known as Guarnerius del Gesù, made in Cremona in 1725. In 2012 the *Folinari* was sold at auction to an anonymous buyer for approximately €1.8 million.

## 4

## The Baron von der Leyen Stradivarius - €2 million

Baron Friedrich Heinrich von Friedrich von der Leyen (1769–1825), a rich German textile merchant, was the owner of this and two other Stradivarius violins. Dating from 1705, it is a true example of a Golden Period Strad. The Norwegian philanthropist Anton Fredrik Klaveness later purchased the violin. It was most recently bought in 2012 by an anonymous buyer for €2 million.

## 3
## The Molitor Stradivarius - €2.5 million

Rumour has it that Napoleon Bonaparte himself was the owner of this 1697 Stradivarius. In fact, it was owned by Juliette Récamier, a famed socialite and prominent figure of the First Empire. In 1804, the violin was passed on to Gabriel Molitor, a general of the Empire. Interestingly, the *Molitor* has had many owners since the end of World War One. In 1989, the American violinist Elmar Oliveira was among its custodians. Of historical significance about Oliveira are two unique projects: a CD released by Bein & Fushi of Chicago, with him performing on some fifteen Stradivari and fifteen Guarneri; and a CD of short pieces highlighting the Library of Congress's collection of rare violins. Five years later, he exchanged it for Albert Stern's *Lady Stretton* Guarneri del Gesù. Violinist Anne Akiko Meyers purchased it for $3.6 million. She also plays the *Royal Spanish* Stradivarius, and the *Vieuxtemps* Guarneri del Gesù. The buyer of the *Vieuxtemps*, who remains anonymous, has given Meyers use of the violin for life.

## — 2 —
## Vieuxtemps" Guarneri del Gesù, - €11 million

*photo courtesy of Anne Akiko Meyers*

This is the del Gesù which has no other comparison. When asked what it is like to play this extraordinary instrument for life, Anne Akiko Meyers said:

There was a depth to the sound that was so profound that I felt like I was a sailboat on top of a vast ocean of colour – and it was my responsibility to try and bring out as much colour and power as it gave me. In particular, the violin has a colossal range. I found I could play the entire repertoire, from Vivaldi to Sibelius to modern works, just on this one violin. All the pieces I've dreamt about being able to accomplish are now within my reach! It feels as though there's colour in my fingertips: when I was recording Vivaldi's Four Seasons it was as though the violin's tone could emulate lightning, drunkenness, birds chirping and the rain pattering down. As for the projection: I never have to worry about playing a pianississimo in a large concert hall, because I know it'll just float to the back without being swallowed up. It's like Kryptonite! It's got power and range, and I feel like it covers the most extreme dimensions of color. Like dark and white chocolate, or the feeling of both the earth and sky in one small instrument. I can't think of any limitations. It's a daring, bold, and innovative violin. It loves playing a very diverse repertoire and feels like the sound is in hi-def or 3D surround sound. This instrument will hopefully live on for many more centuries.

And here she is again, that marvellous Lady....

## — 1 —
## The Lady Blunt Stradivarius - €11 million

This record-breaking violin was sold for £84,000 at Sotheby's in 1971, with the auction house calling on Yehudi Menuhin to demonstrate the quality of the violin. Forty years later, in 2011, the violin was once again put up for auction, by Tarisio, this time to help raise funds for two organisations involved in providing relief to victims of the natural disasters in Japan. It exceeded the record set by the *Molitor*, reaching £9.8 million, more than €11 million. The reason for this ridiculous price? Firstly, the exceptional condition of the instrument; made in 1721 by Antonio Stradivari, during his Golden Period, The *Lady Blunt* has passed from collector to collector ensuring that it has remained in almost original condition. It has hardly been played and so was not subject to the alterations seen in most eighteenth century violins. From the hands of French luthier Jean-Baptiste Vuillaume it passed to Lady Anne Blunt in the mid-nineteenth century. It is she, daughter of Ada Lovelace and granddaughter of Lord Byron, who gives the precious violin its nickname. After *The Red Violin*, this leading lady violin could star in her own film. She's certainly got the curves and the price tag. Such a master violin "has been photographed from more angles than a porn star," says Laurie Niles, a concert violinist and the editor-in-chief of Violinist.com.

By comparison, when evaluating the 23% IRR annual return on the value of a Gerhard Richter painting, *Abstraktes Bild*, purchased for $3.4 million by the guitarist Eric Clapton in 2001, and sold on October 12, 2012 for $32.4, the IRR of the Lady Blunt from 1971 for £84,000 to £9.8 million in 2011, a forty-year investment, averaged a 24.5% IRR. The average IRR for stock markets is 10%. Taking care of such a lady is very much high maintenance. How do you protect such a good investment? Protection and conservation are key considerations when investing in rare instruments. But above all else comes passion.

Bruno Price and Ziv Arazi of Rare Violins of New York and In Consortium explain why long-term investing is the best advice for investing in rare instruments:

> The problem is we are living in a different time. In the same way we press buttons and get answers to everything, the investors will ask what will it do in three years if I sell it, five years if we're lucky, ten years maybe, no one thinks of forty years. The thing that keeps them in the investment is the passion for the players.
>
> At this point virtually every Stradivari violin is known. If one shows up unexpectedly it is more likely to have been stolen than be a previously unknown example.
>
> For lesser makers that carry old certificates of authenticity we always assess them independently of old documentation. There is a lot more known about some of these makers today than even thirty years ago. We have the ability to pull up dozens of photographs in seconds to compare details, whereas in the past a dealer may have relied solely on the opinion of a respected expert of the day who might have a photographic memory but is limited by the quantity of instruments seen.

Christopher Marinello can help provide these photographs. He is the CEO of Art Recovery International which has dedicated databases focused solely on tracking stringed instruments for dealers, auction houses, collectors and buyers, police, museums, insurance companies, and anyone else with an interest in their recovery.

> The most important element from a protection viewpoint would be provenance. You can't protect a rare instrument or even a work of art from being claimed by someone else unless the item you purchased has an impeccable provenance. One could lose their entire investment if the instrument or musical score was stolen or looted. This would be closely followed by authenticity and condition. Every purchase should include an independent report of authenticity and an assessment of condition. It is impossible to protect something that is fraudulent or that is so fragile or heavily restored that it affects its very essence.

Some instruments are never seen again. Others were rumoured to go down with the ship only to resurface. One of the most intriguing is the *Hartley* Stradivarius, the very instrument played on the *Titanic* as it sank in 1912 and auctioned 101 years later for £1.1 million in 2013. The violin was preserved in Hartley's cork and linen backpack, strapped to his back as he drowned. The seawater remarkably did not adversely impact the wood of the violin as the animal glue that was used to hold the leather violin case together only melts when it is hot, not when it is cold. The violin was authenticated and restored. It lived another day to sing its song: "Nearer My God to Thee."

So why would anyone want to invest in something that can be stolen or sunk? As we saw from the *Lady Blunt*, for profit, of course.

## *Alternative investment asset: big notes*

In today's economy, where investments in stocks, bonds, commodities, real estate and hedge funds have either been severely battered or are at record highs and possibly poised for declines, investors are increasingly seeking non-correlated alternative investments.

You need big notes to buy these big names. £11 million is now the standard for such exquisite instruments. Given these prices, it seems only the rich may be able to benefit from such an investment. Philanthropy or portfolio diversification, or pure passion, play a role in these purchases. Though historically rare violins have not been as widely seen as assets for investment as contemporary art or vintage cars, they are gaining significant interest due to the steady increase in value, a finite supply and emerging collector markets in China, India and Russia. Rare string instruments offer a beneficial option to increase an investment portfolio while achieving exceptional long-term appreciation.

To purchase a rare instrument requires research. Over the past twenty years, many rare instruments in the top tier category have increased in value 15% or more per annum, with virtually no downside volatility. Information on individual instruments is available to interested investors and subscribers at https://tarisio.com/cozio-archive/, detailing rare instrument sales going back almost to their date of creation – including Cremonese makers Stradivari, and Guarneri del Gesù, but also Carlo Bergonzi and Guadagnini, Venetians Domenico Montagnana and Matteo Goffriller (primarily makers of cellos). The data reveals one of the few investments where verifiable price information is available over a 200-year period. The Amati website https://amati.com/en/ also offers articles on makers and auction sales records. The Red Book http://theredbook.us publishes the sales of all auctions in the violin trade.

To demonstrate the exponential increase in the value of these instruments, bear in mind that in the previous five years, sales between $6 million and $10 million are common. Many of these same instruments were purchased in the 1960s and 1970s for less than $200,000. Economic downturn does not seem to have any impact on the rise in prices, and reports indicate prices are continuing to increase.

If that does not interest an investor, it would be difficult to understand what would. Few equities deliver such an annual increase without being subject to market pressure. Even the gold standard cannot compare. The only dangers are damage to the instrument, unknown restorations to the instrument or inauthenticity upon purchase.

## *Investing in immortality*

Benjamin Franklin said, "An investment in knowledge pays the best interest." It can also pay for immortality. Investing in immortality means living forever by ensuring your name lives on. Imagine indefinite interest payments with no capital gains tax. Normal investing might make you famous indeed. Few will forget a name like Warren Buffett 100 years from now, just as we study today what Andrew Carnegie or John Rockefeller did over 100 years ago.

This book offers advice from modern day Rockefellers. This rare breed of people are the ones who can make a difference in the valuation, preservation, performance and return on investment of any rare string instrument purchase. They may often describe themselves only as custodians, but they understand how important immortality is to the buyer. They are the best advisors for learning how to invest in a rare instrument.

## *How to invest in a rare instrument*

There are a variety of ways and means of acquiring a rare instrument as an investment asset. Provenance is the purchasing priority. Provenance has power. The authenticity must be verified.

You will be the investor. This book will be your private consultation with the experts in the field who can provide all the necessary advice and authenticity required to feel confident to make such an expensive but profitable investment. However, I must add, use this book only as a resource. Eye to eye, hand to hand and lawyer to lawyer are the recommended approaches.

Where to start? As with all investment, analysis and research are required. The best place is the Museo del Violino in, naturally, Cremona. Virginia Villa, the Director of the Museum shared her insights about the museum for the curious investor.

> We are a museum, to preserve the museum of Cremona where the instruments are born. We have a major responsibility to preserve them. Not to sell them. We determine the conditions of performance. The history is more important. The museum can seek a Galeria with diverse instruments in representing the grand masters – Ruggeri, Bergonzi, Amati, Stradivari of course. And after. This is an important thing, the division sharing of the private and the public visitors. We are informational and educational. Today, the museums are not created to sell instruments.
>
> Of course we have to check the good integrity of the instrument, the history, the scientific proof. We have a commission of experts, not only Cremonese. We work with Charles Beare and other experts, working together. The analysis of sound is also fundamental and musicians assist in the process.
>
> It all began with the first Stradivari in 1961. The commission was composed by two scientists but one musician, Franzetti from La Scala. it sees all aspects of authenticity, varnish, sound, etc.
>
> We are also concerned with conservation. We work with the carabinieri, who are particularly acting to

protect. They control the instruments. Every time we make an exhibition, we work with them, we speak with the Ministry of Culture. Nowadays, there is an easier control only about public property. The private control is difficult. It is easier when the instruments are on exhibition. Also we ask some private owners because it is important to reconstruct periods or style, so there is a need for control.

This is an important moment to have a catalogue of all the instruments. We don't even really know how many there are at the moment; It is difficult to know what is the real definition of a Strad; many instruments are made of different parts. What's important is for us to be clear. This is not always done. Why?

Because of the value of the market. A completely made violin is different if made in parts.

In Italy, the community of violin makers is important. They do a lot to know more about the instruments. Sometimes it is not so clear, because when the market is operating in a very strong way, with great value, you have to be careful. But I think the community knows much more than what is written. So for example, when someone comes to give us a violin, to see an instrument, it is not so difficult to know where it comes from, because the community is very active. It is a closed community, and you can imagine why. The commercial part is important and active, as we know. So, if there is a private donor who wants to buy an instrument to give to the museum, we can participate to the analysis. Also, there are catalogues that are not in public disposal. Like Beare, who are printing the catalogue of all instruments. But they are not a museum, they are a company. And a company seeks profit.

There is indeed profit in the purchasing of a rare instrument, for both dealer and buyer. Once the investor is armed with information, the best way of purchasing is through respectable private dealers such as J & A Beare in London or Rare Violins of New York / In Consortium or Bein & Fushi in Chicago or Eduard Wulfson in Geneva. Auction houses such as Tarisio also participate in the upscale rare instrument market.

Simon Morris of J & A Beare offers advice for the investor interested in purchasing a rare instrument through private dealers or via a public auction:

> The highest quality instruments in the finest condition are the ones that have become more and more rare. Why do they become more rare? Over the years the practice of regular excessive polishing of the varnish can lead to the original patina and texture of the original surface being diminished. And then of course there is day to day damage and some occasionally poorly executed repairs. All these factors can lead to a diminution in desirability and therefore it is the purist examples that show the highest investment returns. This top level of quality instrument rarely comes to be offered at auction which is why auction record prices rarely approach the records set through bespoke sales made privately or by established dealers (look at Guarneri del Gesù for example).

Suzanne Fushi is the President of the Stradivari Society in Chicago, founded by her father Geoffrey Fushi, and who presided over Bein & Fushi, one of the legendary dealers in rare instruments. Many an investor and collector have come to Bein & Fushi. Suzanne gives her advice for the beginning investor in string instruments:

> Authenticity, sound, how responsive is the instrument to a particular musician's playing style. In the case of a collector there are different considerations. I would advise acquiring an instrument by the top maker in their price range, a fine model by the maker, the condition

of the instrument is also important. It sounds simple, but choose a violin that speaks to you, that you have an affinity for. I have a friend who is an extraordinary violinist, we've always shown her the best violins that come through the shop, so she's seen many of the finest violins ever made. She fell in love with an early Stradivari, not his finest example, but perfect for her. That was the right violin for her to pursue.

As the Director of Tarisio Auction House, Jason Price advises clients and collectors on what to consider before bidding on and buying a rare instrument as an alternative investment asset or passion purchase.

Authenticity. Don't buy something of disputed or incomplete authorship. Avoid composites, avoid fringe makers.

Quality of example. Buy the best examples. I'd rather an investor bought an exceptional Grancino than a middling Stradivari.

Condition. Avoid post-cracks to the back. Avoid worm damage in the wrong places.

Provenance. Historical ownership adds intangible value.

Time. Don't expect a quick return, plan to own and enjoy the instrument for 5–15 years.

There are also funds created by corporations, foundations, governments and individuals acquiring instruments for a variety of reasons. Some, like the Stradivari Museo del Violino in Cremona, have a mission to preserve art, antiquities and treasures of national identity. Others, like the Stradivari Society, the Stradivari Trust and the Nippon Foundation exist to provide instruments to younger artists who cannot afford them, for investment returns, and others for a combination of all of these objectives.

If an individual rare instrument is purchased by one buyer through a dealer or auction house, the advantage is not having to share the cost or investment value with anyone else. The downside is being sure of the conditions and provenance because challenges to authenticity can create a major difference between the purchase price and the instrument's real value. Physical conditions are also paramount to consider, checking any history of maintenance or restoration, insurance policies, and the provenance of previous owners and players, though not necessarily contingent to the sale. Simon Morris says:

> It is important that an instrument is well looked after in order to retain value. That generally means minimal interference and no invasive polishing. There is no harm in letting the instrument rest in a cupboard for a generation so that future violinists can enjoy it in the same condition as it is today. An instrument certainly becomes more sellable with a provenance that includes a famous player, such as the *Milstein* Strad we sold some years ago. There is no rule of thumb to the value a famous player's name might add but it certainly makes a difference. But I have to add that a remarkable example that turns up with little or no provenance is still a remarkable violin – in some ways the fact that it is a discovery could add to the fascination.

Eduard Wulfson, regarded by many as among the world's most significant dealers and pedagogues, offers his perspective:

> For the investor, the expected rate of increase in the value of the instrument is enhanced when it is played by a star soloist. And for that musician, being able to express a top interpretation, deploying the sophisticated sound of one of the finest stringed-instruments in the world, helps them to grasp their destiny. The star soloist offers attractiveness to buy, not necessarily increasing

> the value. I had an experience selling instruments to a collector, far from music, but he had a passion for art but no real knowledge of music, but his best friend was a musician and he had one of the most prestigious collections in the world. My advice is great musicians must be present in front of the investor to release the energy to purchase this beautiful instrument. Because in this respect people know the investment is sure.

Many investors buy equities or investments through a money manager or stockbroker. Buying a rare instrument from a private dealer allows these experts to do more than advise on the purchase, as would a broker. They are the conduit to ensure the instrument is put in the hands of the right artist who would add profile and profit to the investment.

Wulfson adds more in his own colourful Russian accent:

> Someone from the tribe of Aborigines was listening to Mozart Piano Concerto, K488, 2nd movement. The Chief was asked what he felt. He said: "What I feel is the truth." At this moment they understand what is the truth they will follow. The instrumentalists mastering our instruments come first and then only after can the truth be told. This ethical preparation is required to merit the truth. Classical musicians often put themselves in danger to have a career through corruption. Mediocrity spoils the career. Things have to be sorted out in natural selection, cleaned up. Clean the group that is at the highest level: Clean the garden. I don't mean to be Maximalist, even putting less level than the genius of Kubrick, etc. Not everyone can play like Heifetz or Menuhin or even Lozakovitj, Barati or Conunova. Our duty is that instrumentalists on string instruments have to have the phenomenal approach to mastering the instrument that open the mouth of the genius. Then truth can be told. Then truth can only be compared with the voice of genius.

To touch genius is quite a personal incentive to invest. It also allows the owner to have his or her name forever associated with both the genius who made the violin and the other genius who plays it. What then? Should it be sold or given to another soloist as many have done? Is a Strad or del Gesù governed by the same investment strategies that someone like Warren Buffett might have: Sell high, buy low? In the case of violins, rarely does an authentic instrument like a Strad have a low valuation. If it is real, the value only goes up. When is the right time to receive that return on investment?

In order to recoup the investment, the instrument will have to be sold, often with a significant dealer commission ranging from 5–20% of the sale price. The longer the appreciation, the higher the resale value. But, of course, an investor must have the reserves available to purchase a rare instrument and that can be expensive.

But there is another way.

Add a quasi-charitable component to your purchase and find either a soloist who buys back your appreciated invested shares or perhaps find a middle-aged artist with a valuable instrument. By offering to purchase half the instrument at a slight discount, creating liquidity for the artist, it allows them to continue to use it until they retire. At that time, you own a piece of the instrument and could acquire the rest of the instrument or sell it.

Nigel Brown OBE created the Stradivari Trust specifically for this purpose. He recognised the need among young professional soloists to play on outstanding rare instruments, despite their inability to own them. Most soloists have had to rely on the largesse of individual owners, foundations or societies, like the Stradivari Society in Chicago. Not all players can have access to these instruments or are considered worthy by the artistic committees who determine the benefitting musician. In the case of the Stradivari Trust, it is exclusive to British string players. The investor philanthropic scheme creates a consortium of investors, buying shares as one would in an equity. Brown explains:

> A musician will usually come to me having fallen in love with an instrument. What I do is gather a group of people – professionals, the kind you would expect to see at chamber music concerts at the Wigmore Hall – prepared to put up the money and form a syndicate, rather like you would for a racehorse. We then set up a bare trust [which HMRC defines as "one in which each beneficiary has an immediate and absolute right to both capital and income"] and go out on the stump with a selling document that describes the instrument, the musician and what their need is and how the trust works, and try to find "investors".

According to Allianz Musical Insurance (AMI), there is an increasing trend of investors joining to form syndicates that pool assets in order to buy rare instruments. AMI worked with Emotional Assets Management and Research (EAMR), an investment advisory boutique, on a report in 2009, which showed that fine musical investment funds are returning between 12% a year. According to the EAMR prospectus:

> The Fund seeks to provide qualified investors with an opportunity to achieve long-term capital appreciation through investment in Emotional Assets. Its objective is to deliver a stable target growth rate of 15% per annum, with predictable volatility – at the same time preserving capital. The Guernsey domiciled Fund will employ no leverage and is unique in that it will allow investors to benefit from a broad and diversified exposure to Emotional Assets – the first time that this has been achievable via a single fund vehicle.

Bernard Duffy, the former managing director of EAMR says:

> Smart investors are looking to their emotional assets as safe havens and a long-term store of value. We are seeing

> more and more high net investors, their advisors and family offices look to musical investments as long-term stores of value, as well as other emotional assets [...] We believe that the worlds of collecting and investing are converging and this phenomenon will attract more investors into this space. This will mean more fine and rare musical instrument investment funds, which are likely to lead to continued price escalation of these instruments over the medium to long-term.

As with the Stradivari Trust, these funds, foundations or syndicates then loan out their investment to young or established soloists, in the hope of furthering their musical careers and enhancing the value of the instrument in the process. The Rare Violins In Consortium is such an instrument fund with this very purpose.

The famous Israeli-American soloist, Gil Shaham, was loaned a 1719 Golden Period Stradivarius from the Rare Violins In Consortium investment pool. Shaham is not the only beneficiary, but certainly the most recent to benefit from this philosophy of instrument value enhancement. Shaham says in *The Strad* magazine:

> I am very grateful to the anonymous benefactor and Rare Violins In Consortium for the use of this Stradivari violin... playing this remarkable violin is life-changing for people like myself. Imagine being given a new voice... imagine finding you can say things differently and even say different things... hats off to this organization and its supporters for improving musicians' lives.

Founded in 2018 by Bruno Price and Ziv Arazi from Rare Violins of New York, In Consortium was established to provide the infrastructure to allow donors, investors and collectors the synergy to find the best soloists to increase the value and reputation of both the instrument and the investment pool.

Bruno Price and Ziv Arazi explain:

> In Consortium was started as a way to get more great instruments into the hands of more great players. There are people who own fine instruments who have been nervous about loaning them out, but we are here to make sure the instruments are diligently matched with responsible and deserving talent and are properly cared for, insured and maintained… In Consortium is essentially the buffer and conduit to make this happen with surety. In addition on a business level, by loaning their fine instruments to musicians, benefactors are also provided with a number of ways to reduce their cost of ownership and increase the long-term realization of their investment.

Shaham's name is in the exclusive circle of the greatest living violinists, as are Maxim Vengerov, Anne Sophie Mutter, Itzhak Perlman, Daniel Hope and Leonidas Kavakos, among a few others not named. They will already be remembered for their musical legacy in as much as the investor donor or the investment syndicate will be forever honoured for their generosity.

Bruno and Ziv continue:

> The value only increases if the players name is of importance to the next owner. The 1719 Stradivari has a relatively short history in that there were only three owners since 1937. It was not owned by a renowned player so its current owner believes that it will carry Gil Shaham's name in the future. For us one of the crucial attributes of a recipient is that they are good people – after all we have to deal with them. Generally, if they are honest players who have integrity in their music making, and who respect their fellow musicians and themselves, then they are very likely to respect the instrument they play and will look after it. Beyond that we have to be

confident that the instrument is not only a good match for the player, but that it will inspire them to search for a greater sound palette and develop their presence and communication. Developing artists are certainly the most exciting to follow, but there are a few great players who are still searching for a "new voice" that cannot afford the level of instrument that they need.

After a few days with the 1719 Stradivari, Gil proclaimed that it was life changing, how could anyone not get excited at the prospect of hearing him playing with a renewed freshness and inspired energy?

The Stradivari Society is a division of Bein & Fushi Rare Violins. Suzanne Fushi shares a similar mission of supporting developing soloists:

I've found that all of our patrons have a few things in common; the love of classical music and violins in particular, and a philanthropic spirit, and a belief in the importance of supporting our next generation of artists. We loan our instruments out on a yearly basis, the artist agrees to bring them to a restorer of our designation three times a year to ensure that they are being kept in excellent shape and to handle any required maintenance. Some of the most pristine instruments should be conserved and actually do belong in museums, but these violins were made to be played and the majority of them belong in the hands of artists who will do their utmost to maintain them.

Jason Price at Tarisio offers an overview of the investor and collector market:

The market has created several ingenious vehicles for investing in instruments over the past few decades. The most significant are the private wealth funds and foundations like the Nippon Music Foundation, the Austrian National Bank, Dextra Musica, the Chi Mei Foundation, Samsung etc. who own impressive collections of historical instruments generally intended to be loaned to promising players. Next comes private patrons including wealthy families and individuals. Syndicated trusts like those put together by Nigel Brown have created a community of supporters and enabled fractional participation–you no longer need millions to own a "share" of a Stradivari. These trusts also encourage the musicians themselves to own shares. Finally are the clubs and consortiums of instrument owners like the Stradivari Society which add a social element to instrument ownership.

The Nippon Foundation in Japan shares the same investment and distribution philosophy. Tamio Kano is the Managing Director. He describes the Nippon way:

> I think this depends on the purpose of the instrument purchase. A performer would choose an instrument that is compatible with their sound, bowing, and fingering style. An investor or other temporary owners would choose an instrument that they think would increase in value over a short period of time. Since the Nippon Music Foundation first decided to conserve Stradivarius and other instruments, we planned to loan these instruments gratis to musicians, so we have abided by the following guidelines/conditions:
>
> - The instrument is in an excellent condition and suitable for concert activities.
> - The instrument is recognised to be a world cultural asset that must be preserved.
> - The instrument has a good provenance and is confirmed to be genuine.

- The price of the instrument is fair and in line with the market price.
- We do not pursue instruments wanted by other musicians.

These five guidelines have not changed since we first began our instrument preservation and loan project. As we are a Public Interest Incorporated Foundation authorised by the Japanese Government, instrument purchases are determined through a resolution passed by our board of trustees and counsellors.

Our Foundation does not plan on selling instruments, so I do not know if loaning them to a renowned musician would contribute to its increase in monetary value. However, when our Foundation purchased instruments, the fact that a renowned musician had been using it in the past did serve as a guarantee that it would be an instrument that produced a wonderful sound.

We at the Nippon Music Foundation hold around ten concerts a year featuring our instruments and loan recipients. This includes chamber music concerts with over ten of our loan recipients, as well as recitals and orchestral collaborations. We ask our instrument loan recipients to perform in these concerts up to five times a year.

In loaning our instruments, we ask perspective loan recipients to apply by submitting the required documents and most recent video recordings of their performances. The Instrument Loan Committee then meets to carefully deliberate and determine whether the loan can be approved. In this case, the maximum loan period is seven years, and there is an age limit to apply. Other than this, we also loan an instrument to the Grand Prize winner of the quadrennial Queen Elizabeth Violin Competition, for four years until the next Violin Competition is held. We also have a category in which we loan our instruments for under a year to those who

> wish to use them for a specific performance (such as a debut or anniversary concert) or for a recording.
>
> The purpose of our Foundation's instrument loan project is primarily to support young musicians.

Long-term investing is the mantra of most successful investors. Investing in rare instruments can take years for a large return, but so, too, a career of a soloist. Combining the arc of a soloist's maturation and success with the appreciation of a rare instrument is a unique and ideal way of maximising a return on investment. Sir Nigel Brown elaborates:

> We set up these trusts with a time period of between ten and twenty years depending on the age of the individual. When you get to the end of the period, if the musician hasn't made it, then the instrument is put on the market and sold, unless by going on bended knee to the contributors the musician can persuade them to extend the life of the trust.

What is the benefit for such a consortium scheme if not money?

> It is a huge treat to be able to help a musician, to see someone whom one has helped really blossom. The right instrument can really open up his or her playing. A young musician can experience a step change in their career as a result of having a better instrument. The instrument benefits, the player benefits, and, with any luck, the philanthro-investor will too.

Bruno Price and Ziv Arazi describe their method of investing and loaning:

> We find that the most important consideration is what the motivation for the purchase really is. If it's purely

a financial investment, then the level of trust with the dealer needs to be very high. Authenticity and truthful representation are critical. If important details are overlooked and the investor is enthusiastically promised a profit with a quick return it often ends with disappointment. The instruments in the collection of In Consortium are legally owned by their owners and we coordinate the loan, insurance and maintenance. Occasionally there has been an extraordinary instrument that has come on the market that we feel would be so well suited to a particular player and could dramatically impact his or her life and career. The challenge then was to find a sponsor with the same vision who had the financial capability to purchase it. There are not enough people like this so we are always looking to expand the number.

We only take on instruments that we know intimately. As we are responsible to the player for the reliability of the instrument we need to have full confidence in its condition and stability. Initial funding of In Consortium came from Rare Violins of New York otherwise the objective is for the program to be self-sufficient. Insurance costs are covered by the player, which assures the owners of the player's commitment. Regular inspections and check-ups ensure that the instrument is being looked after and that it is functioning optimally. Our workshop is one of the finest in the world which gives complete assurance to both the owners and players.

Jonathan Moulds, as a collector expert, owns one of the most famed collections of rare violins in the world, including three of possibly the best examples of Stradivarius ever made as well as an equally fine example of a Guarneri violin. He comments during our interview on the question of consortiums:

> I think consortiums can be very effective but I have purchased individually to date. Given the value of many of the great instruments, it is often more effective for a player to seek out a number of like-minded individuals to invest in an instrument, particularly if an investor is new to the market. I can imagine that individuals, as a part of the right consortium, can have both an artistically rewarding time as well as financially rewarding investment and contribute greatly to the careers of a series of artists.

As previously noted, Nigel Brown founded the Stradivari Trust to benefit UK instrumentalists. It is a model that could be emulated elsewhere in other countries, especially in Asia, which is an emerging market for soloists. While the best soloists in the world might have a permanent loan of a master instrument, or the funds to actually afford to buy, the majority of soloists who need an instrument rely on such investment schemes. For an investor, it is a less expensive approach to such an alternative investment asset, with many of the same benefits as owning it outright. The point is the instrument not only has a home, but the hands to bring out its fullest potential.

Brown offers the incentive and investor wisdom:

> If you can't raise the money you can't get the instruments. I can cope with one at a time. The time scale can get drawn out. Going back a few years, I got a Montagnana cello for Steven Isserlis. It came from Martin Lovett. It was expensive. Some people don't like dealing with dealers. My experience is private individuals are more expensive than dealers. No support. Will they take the instrument back? No. Will they pay for repairs? If you buy from a dealer, you get that all that stuff.
>
> So I got to the last fifty grand. I'd shaken every tree. I rang up Martin, and I said I can't get the other

50. I asked: "Would you want to retain some interest in the instrument?" He said, "Why would I?" I said: "If you keep the 50 grand, you could give it to your grandchildren." "And why would I do that?" he replied. So I said: "Well, the great thing about giving them a share in the instrument is they can't spend it."

He loved the idea and retained the small chunk. That's the wonderful point about the syndicated instrument. The people go along and hear the violin or cello or whatever. And go to the green room and introduce themselves. Nice to meet you. You know I have a piece of your instrument?

As a luthier, Florian Leonhard naturally advocates the playing of the instrument.

Use improves a violin because the constant vibrations make the wood more resonant. Is there a perfect age for a violin to be heard at its best? Maybe there might be such a date. It is irrelevant. It is still a young wine even after 300 years.

And yet, a violin is still a piece of wood. The sound may be abstract and ephemeral, but could the instrument itself also be subject to the ravages of time?

Leonhard gives his perspective about the fragility and force of the instrument:

An old Amati from 1660 or all the others are super strong, even older than Strad and they are strong and rich and deep and sonorous. Even if twenty years after it would die, it is not to be concerned. Like old buildings 2000 years old, the beams are amazing. Wood is incredible material. Nature has created it for hundreds of millions of years, that last. What we create doesn't last twenty years. Think plastic on the beach. The plastic disintegrates, the wood doesn't. The wood is treated on the Strad. When I make my violins, in my many years of research on long term longevity of ground and varnish. I learned this. I see this problem of material also in many good violin makers of the early twentieth century. I didn't want to do this. I was surrounded by the greatest instruments ever created, and then see other violins having no value. I don't want to be one of those others because they sound brittle and sharp. The treatment of wood and varnish turned hard and like a glass layer on the violin. I was trying to create in my research some material when it is at its driest point making the softest resonant quality. That is what I observed about the Cremonese. The wood remained soft. The Milanese and Napolitano, like Gagliano, don't have the same cache of sound and therefore do not demand the prices.

Jonathan Moulds responds:

Firstly, I think the comment from Florian Leonhard is relevant with the vast majority of instruments. Instruments where possible should be played by musicians rather than locked away. They bring tremendous pleasure to many music lovers across the world. My only caveat is the following – some instruments have such exceptional condition and essentially are timepieces to history. These instruments are few and far between. At even the very highest end of the market, with both Stradivarius and del Gesù instruments, the majority can be played regularly by soloists and other performers and an owner would have no concerns about any detriment to value. For the very select view, significantly less regular performance would keep an instrument's condition at an exceptional level. Analogies with other asset classes may appear crudely simplistic but on the same basis, you would not drive a Ferrari GTO on a very regular basis.

Though driving the Ferrari with a Strad in the car is quite a delicious thought. Just keep to the speed limit and don't cross the border, though, unless you have the provenance, papers and passport. Yes, rare instruments have their own passport.

## *Return on Investment: Money and Music*

Traveling with a string instrument has become a full-time sport, with reports of damaged violins and broken bows by the dozen. Not to mention confiscated because of ivory inlaid on the fiddle or the bow. The bows may have to have a CITES certificate, meaning obtaining the Convention on International Trade of Endangered Species document, proving any ivory or other banned body-parts were not acquired after February 26, 1976. These permits are either renewed each time they travel or a multi-year passport can be issued. Pianos have been forced to remove ivory keys. With respect to the string instrument, the idea of removing the ivory inlaid of the Stradivarius *Messiah* would be sacrilegious; hence, the passport. Think two first class seats for that cello and the player. Otherwise, that investment might be worthless if left to the luggage handlers. Buying the instrument is one thing. Keeping the instrument intact is another. Both are costly, but doing it right can literally mean the difference between profit and loss, and profit they certainly can.

Moulds, who is a serious collector, and also an accomplished violinist who has played with the London Symphony Orchestra and on whose board he now sits, has no doubt of the investment value of his collection, both personal and professional.

> They've been a spectacularly good investment. My violins have tripled in value every fifteen years, and I expect they will continue to outperform with growing demand from Asia. This asset class seems to me unique. It allows an owner to be philanthropic and still make a financial return which has exceeded almost (and maybe) all other

> mainstream asset classes when looked over the medium and longer term. I did not initially purchase with the goal of making significant financial returns. I have been educated over years on the financial attractiveness of instruments. For me it was a passion. I suppose many entrepreneurs who are financially successful would take the same view of their businesses.

Jonathan Moulds purchased his first violin over twenty years ago. At that time prices were still expensive but not exorbitant. Working as the head of International Global Markets business for Bank of America, he went to an American dealer he found listed on the early days of the internet. Carrying his dream to buy a good violin once he had made money, he intended to "buy a second-hand Porsche." Instead, after being convinced by the expertise and research of the dealer, he bought a Guadagnini. The rest was history. A year later he purchased a Stradivarius.

> Bear in mind, even then, the Guadagnini was significantly more expensive than I expected. I did not buy for appreciation. But I did buy a Stradivarius a year later. How did I learn about the investment potential? It happened because I got a call from the dealer who said he had an offer to buy the Strad. I said, why would I do that? I just bought it a year ago. The offer was 1 million above what I paid for it. Me being a banker, I was cynical and thought about this person having an agenda. Get me a lawyer's letter for the commitment to buy, I said. I got the letter and I though ok, maybe I should buy some more. I didn't sell it. I just wanted to know it could be sold.

Not all purchases are investment related. The benefits are an afterthought. Julian Lloyd-Webber, has played the 1690 *Barjansky* Stradivarius cello since he purchased it at an auction in 1983. His motivation was musical, not for investment purposes. However, today he says,

> I have played it for nearly thirty years now. It is my "sound" and we have shared some fantastic moments together. I know that it has increased hugely in value since 1983. This level of instrument is in very short supply and they will always hold and increase their value. If the market dips in the West there will always be buyers in the East, and you cannot say that about property!

Indeed, as Moulds points out:

> A violin is a global asset. Whatever the assets are, individuals buy in different jurisdictions. From a taxation perspective, with instruments they are global assets. While people might want to buy in dollars, currencies do move. Therefore, what looks expensive in one currency may not be in another. Clearly if you buy a house in the USA, the cost is what it is. If you buy the instrument that cost is transferrable.

So, then, whether you are in Geneva, London, Moscow or Shanghai, let us talk about provenance and prices.

Jonathan Moulds knows valuation better than most:

> I think that provenance is important but this adds to the value over many decades. Indeed, a number of instruments have been named (or had one name added) to reflect an owner or player who is now regarded as historically very relevant. There are a number of instruments *ex-Kreisler* for example. The main value of a dated instrument from any maker comes mainly from condition and the relevant period of the maker's life when it was made. Stradivarius lived well into his nineties and made instruments throughout his adult life. The style of instrument changed through different periods, and today the most valuable instruments are generally made

during the first twenty-two years of the year 1700 which is regarded as his Golden Period. Having said that, the condition of an instrument makes a very significant difference, and there are certainly instruments outside his Golden Period that can fetch very high sums and, also a fair amount of variation on prices of instruments made during even his Golden Period.

Eduard Wulfson takes the issue of provenance more personally:

For provenance, we make sure of the certification of authenticity, we make sure to express ourselves to stand by the deal. For example: I sell you a Strad violin and you want to sell it. I would work with you, buy shares, buy back or offer consignment; This reassurance is important to the client.

To protect the price, not an auction which is between wholesale and retail to the professionals. There is a limit on the ethics, so I would always like to know if it is a private person who sells or a professional. In auction to have an understanding who sold what. We find out and I send my people to research what is the provenance.

10% increase in insurance. If we sell for 20 million, insurance would agree to insure for 22 million, 5–10%, depends on the insurance valuation. Then the title goes to the buyer with full payment.

Normally I would ask two experts to determine the judgement of the price. Then insurance may agree or not, but normally they would agree. It is up to the client's decision to wish or not. It is a negotiation matter. I never insist anything. I propose a menu of possibilities and advising which way. The final decision goes to the advisors of the client and to the client himself.

Provenance needs protection. Preserving the investment becomes paramount when it comes to proving provenance.

Failing a stock market crash and bankruptcy, an equity investment is rather sound and stable over the long term. There is money invested. It is all on paper and in portfolios. What would an investor do if their investment gets damaged, stolen, confiscated or even destroyed?

Like the CITES document protecting endangered animals, there is a convention to protect the instruments beyond just inlaid ivory. The 1970 UNESCO convention on the protection of art and antiquities of cultural identity has become a necessary political and diplomatic contract between nations to conserve and preserve these objects designated as heritage for humanity. The "intangible cultural heritage of a country" refers to what has profoundly characterised it culturally and even socially through time. UNESCO states "The intangible cultural heritage is transmitted from generation to generation and is constantly recreated by communities and groups, in response to their environment, their interaction with nature and their history." This means patrimony that has been touching culture for centuries and still does exercise a visible influence on a specific area's way of life, economy, artistic production. The "intangible cultural heritage" helps people connect with their past. UNESCO continues and reinforces their identity and that tradition continues even today.

Ana Luiza Thompson Flores, Director of UNESCO's Regional Bureau for Science and Culture in Europe, rearticulates the UNESCO how and why:

> UNESCO has recognized the importance of this tradition in 2012, when *il saper fare liutario* of Cremona entered its list of the intangible cultural patrimony of the world. The town breathes music through and through: with its 140 *botteghe liutarie* (workshops specializing in the creation of string instruments), it is the only real centre of violin making in the world. The work of Cremona's violin makers is protected by the Consorzio Liutai Antonio Stradivari, which does not only endorse the work of Cremona's violin makers, but

also keeps track of each and every instrument produced to facilitate authentication.

The tradition of Cremonese string instrument making is Inscribed in 2012 (7.COM) on the Representative List of the Intangible Cultural Heritage of Humanity. Cremonese violin craftsmanship is highly renowned for its traditional process of fashioning and restoring violins, violas, cellos and contrabasses. Even today, violin makers attend a specialized school, based on a close teacher-pupil relationship, before being apprenticed in a local workshop, where they continue to master and perfect their techniques – a never-ending process. Each violin maker constructs from three to six instruments per year, shaping and assembling more than seventy pieces of wood around an inner mould by hand, according to the different acoustic response of each piece. No two violins are alike. Every part of the instrument is made with a specific wood, carefully selected and naturally well-seasoned. No semi-industrial or industrial materials are used. Craftsmanship requires a high level of creativity: the craftsperson has to adapt general rules and personal knowledge to every instrument. Cremonese violin makers are deeply convinced that sharing their knowledge is fundamental to the growth of their craftsmanship, and dialogue with musicians is deemed essential so as to understand their needs. It is because of Count Cozio di Salabue, who bought Stradivari's workshop from the master's last son and studied his techniques, that we know how the great violin makers of the past worked. In the 1920s, the di Salabue's family sold Stradivari's workshop and all his material to violin maker Giuseppe Fiorini, who brought Stradivari's standards and knowledge to the twentieth century, the same standards and knowledge UNESCO chose to be part of the world's Intangible Cultural Heritage.

Tamio Kano's philosophy about cultural identity takes on Japanese spiritual dimensions:

> Japan, much like Italy, is a country with a long history and tradition. To live besides various natural environments is to have a mind of reverence for all things. Japanese people feel and find a soul in all things regardless whether they are western, including instruments and music. I think that feeling may be the same in Italy as well.

Faust lost his soul. What happens if your investment is stolen or even confiscated? Who do you call? It would be wise to have Christopher Marinello's number. The CEO of Art Recovery International offers clarity for the concerned investor should any claim or confiscation occur:

> Rare instruments, and even manuscripts and scores can certainly be considered Cultural Property and would come under the purview of existing national laws and international conventions. If stolen, which country's law would apply would depend on the place of theft, where the object was sold, and where it was located. Objects stolen from state museums and libraries could rely on the UNESCO and UNIDROIT treaties and count on assistance from INTERPOL. The intervention of the Carabinieri, FBI, Scotland Yard, and other police forces with an internal art crime team could also be expected depending on the location of the theft and the location of the object.

Provenance and protection should therefore be included in any collection and investment strategy.

Jonathan Moulds elaborates further on the subject of conservation and protection:

> My view is, as with the protection of art and antiquities, as owners we are simply keepers for the next generation

and generations to come. Conservation is very important therefore. It brings me back to my original comment – many fine instruments have had restoration work done and will need restoration work in the future to keep them both performing exceptionally and it is important to retain as many of the original condition features (such as varnish) as possible. Poor work does happen and that is why I think any buyer should ensure that work is carried out by highly experienced restorers who have had many years in the business.

Tamio Kano shares the experience of the Nippon Foundation and the importance of trusting the musicians entrusted to play their collection:

The Foundation carefully instructs loan recipients on the preciousness of these Stradivarius and other instruments at the beginning, so we trust them to take good care of our instruments. As custodian of these instruments, the Foundation assumes insurance costs. In terms of repairs as well, we assume all expenses and mandate that they only take place at our designated luthiers.

Our Foundation issues detailed guidelines to our loan recipients on how **not** to handle our instruments. However, if one of our musicians shows no improvement in their treatment of their instrument after repeated instructions, then we ask them to return the instrument to us at that point.

There are many organizations and individuals all over the world who loan instruments to musicians. I believe each of these organizations and individuals should acquire instruments within their abilities and resources (with regards to price as well as manpower needed for instrument preservation) and strive to conserve and maintain them while loaning them to musicians.

There was one incident when one of our loan recipients damaged the instrument while traveling, but we were able to cover for that with insurance. However, if a damage is clearly caused by the musician either deliberately or through grave negligence, then we ask the musician to repay for the damages.

As for customs confiscation, we had one instrument confiscated at Frankfurt Airport in Germany in September 2012. However, through customs declaration procedures, we were able to have it returned. Since then, whenever our instruments are being taken out of Japan, we have made it a rule to use ATA Carnet documents for Customs declarations.

Our musicians have an obligation as loan recipients to maintain our instruments as well as exercise maximum care and attention, so we have not had an incident up until now where one of our instruments was stolen.

Wulfson argues for the necessity of protection:

I represent the instrument to the buyer with full understanding to the buyer the authenticity in all parts possible, in damages or restoration, conservation, detail explanation of the period, technical abilities, dendrology examination. Only for table of violin, not the back, but if it matches, it's probably authentic. An analysis is to be sure of the period of the wood. If it says nineteenth century, difficult to argue it is a Strad. It is a period of time and comparable vibration of the wood with these makers. Sometimes there is necessity to do a scanner due to fantasy of competition. Damage to wood is another story a scanner will show where damage was and why but also which way the insect came out of the wood. Dendrology and scanner in last years became important to the buyer because there is a mixture. So, also in state of preservation is what we can do, otherwise competitors could make wrong statements to buyer and clients. It's a kind of obsession with the new technology that doesn't

> have any sense, because the instrument itself is built 1700 and onwards to our days, if so well preserved, so small damages of worms or in the wood, doesn't make any sense to exaggerate. It's only disloyal competition that makes destabilization to client's mind to buy or not. In the area of the sound-post in the back, if there is damage, in the back, it could lead to 50% reduction in value of instrument.

Reduction would be only due to damage, but restoration can help restore value. Confiscation cannot. Provenance is also an important detail because your investment just might have a claim from descendants or cultural ministries. What happens if an instrument you own is damaged in transit or confiscated by customs?

Eduard Wulfson recites the mantra of provenance: Certify the authenticity.

> Regarding customs issues, they have nothing to do with ownership. Some musicians were stupid, because instead of declaring customs, if it is lended, to show papers and certificates, what are the terms for concert purpose, etc. In certain countries, it is not needed. Not such a big drama, as a normal customs officer would see it not as a dramatic crime. What they are scared is that you bring a cheap undeclared violin in the country and take out a rare violin. There is no real danger they would take possession. About the criminal offense regarding insurance, if it is stolen, and proven it is not insurance fraud, they pay full price, until the thieves are found. Then insurance owns and then resells. As what happened with Huberman and then to Amadeus Quartet then to Joshua Bell. The Pierre Amoyal story with the 1717 *Kochanski* Stradivarius scandal is very dramatic, but very rare, it is comparable to plane crash. Totally rare.

And, yet, rare does happen. Most recently, in 2019, customs officials at Moscow's Domodedovo airport seized a valuable eighteenth century violin from the Russian violinist Nikolai Managazze, who had returned from his home in Abu Dhabi, having applied to compete in the Tchaikovsky competition. The instrument is on loan from a Swiss Foundation. The Russians have demanded proof that it is not part of their national heritage. The violin stayed in Russian custody for over six months, with the recovery penalty for the violinist not having properly registered the violin from a previous visit going from exceedingly high, nearing $1 million to one that seemed only symbolic, around $9000. The Russian Minister of Culture, Vladimir Medinsky explained the violinist, had "failed to register the violin when he last left Russia, as the rules required. He had only himself to blame." Clearly, the risks for an investor owner loaning an instrument to a soloist are real. Managazze is not a dimwit and probably had good reasons, and the Stifftung are honorable brokers, but it is hard to argue with a Russian customs officer.

Bruno Price and Ziv Arazi give a clear picture about the artist's responsibility:

> Instruments like this never leave the hands of the player. If an accident happens, which is very rare, the insurance company will usually cover repair costs and any depreciation. A player will carry paperwork for the violin that will prevent it from being seized by customs. The few times that this happened in the last years, customs were tracking down people who had not been paying taxes or a couple of times it was simply the customs agent having a bad day. Russia is a particularly difficult country to travel to with an instrument. Everything needs to be registered before going in so that there is proof that it's the same instrument that is leaving the country. If there is a theft it depends where it takes place, but primarily it is the local authorities that are contacted

> first. In most cases of theft, the violin was not taken very far, and it's very rare for a targeted, planned robbery to be successful.

Simon Morris adds:

> Luckily most musicians generally look after instruments like they are a family member and on top of that the insurance policies are very comprehensive. Cultural artifacts: instruments are already protected. In order to sell from country to country you need an export license like any other art work. The Italian rules can be stricter than other countries. The payment of insurance is agreed between owner and borrower. Damage and theft is paid for by insurance. A lender's agreement would cover the arrangements for traveling through customs and some countries might be excluded for travel. I have never known a case of a verified rare instrument being confiscated without being returned.

Florian Leonhard continues:

> Most instruments have some provenance. You are already alerted. If I get a violin that doesn't have a proper provenance, I do so much research. It has never traced back to anything criminal or confiscated. I know a case of a del Gesù in Switzerland. It was not authentic, but he tried to prove to the world it was a del Gesù, and then he was able to sell it for millions. But it was a private person. He made it to be a del Gesù, even if it wasn't. There are people who buy without consulting experts like myself.

These people may regret their investment without the proper provenance. Unless they sell it to another blind buyer. It is obligatory to have full insurance, whether stored in a safe or played by a virtuoso. For sure it cannot be insured if it is not authentic. Maintenance of 300-year-old rare instruments requires insurance. "Annual insurance for a $1 million-plus instrument is at least $4000, which covers being flown to concerts all over the world," says Julia Coakley, divisional director at Lark Insurance Broking Group.

Jonathan Moulds concludes:

> All instruments are fully insured and the premiums for insurance are reasonable. I think this reflects that, while it does happen, few instruments are ultimately lost for posterity. A very small number are stolen and disappear for years but few are lost for ever. In terms of damage, many rare instruments are a number of hundred years old. The conditions we have today – air-conditioned, humidity controlled, excellence in restoration are so far advanced than what would have existed through most of the instrument's life. What is remarkable to me is that most instruments have survived through many of the major conflicts, including of course the two World Wars.

So, the big question is asked: **How much would it cost to purchase a rare instrument today?**

Rare instruments for the "sophisticated investor" and the modern soloist would cost $1 million to $16 million and up.

This range of investment will purchase most anything you desire, from the grandfather of the violin, Nicolo Amati, to the genius of Antonio Stradivari and Joseph Guarneri. This is only for serious collectors and connoisseurs who understand what it means to own one of the finest representations of music and artistic achievement ever made by human hand, and to contribute provenance to both the heritage of the Italian masters and to the greatest performances by world class artists in the finest concert halls and theatres. To own such an instrument allows the investor to essentially choose the soloist who would provide both profile and profit.

Of course, there are master instruments that have never seen an auction block. They are rarely viewed or are on display in a museum. Some are even rumoured not to exist. They are mint condition original instruments, with legendary pedigrees and are still retaining their original necks, cases and bows. They include the finest of the inlaid Stradivarius, the *Messiah*, and Paganini's *Cannon* or *Il Cannone* made by Joseph Guarneri del Gesù.

## *Is it possible to still buy or invest in one of these master instruments?*

In my interviews with the dealer and pedagogue Eduard Wulfson; Simon Morris, Co-Director of J&A Beare in London; Tamio Kano of the Nippon Foundation; Jason Price of Tarisio Auctions; Suzanne Fushi of Bein & Fushi and the luthier and dealer Florian Leonhard, I asked them all the same question: If someone was thinking of investing in a rare instrument, what are the most important points to consider before purchasing either through a private dealer or in auction and are there still any good instruments left to buy?

Simon Morris of J & A Beare is considered by the newspaper the *Independent* as "The Acknowledged World Authority on Stringed Instruments". With co-director Steven Smith, J & A Beare continues to attract the highest levels of buyers and sellers and soloists.

Smith was quoted in an article by Lydon White in *Billionaire* magazine reprinted on their company website:

> Fortunately, I don't think violins have generally been bought purely for speculative purposes, which is fantastic because the best hands for a great violin are those of a great player. Players generally find sponsors to support them by buying and then lending a violin. The sponsor gets a great investment at the same time

> and is not just a purely speculative buyer who is only investing… We had some of the best business ever in the recent depression. We found that in 2008 there was panic and people didn't know where to put their money. They came to us wanting to buy violins because they can be carried anywhere in the world and sold anywhere in the world in any currency, and in that sense, they are quite phenomenal investments.

Simon Morris elaborated more on the subject in our interview:

> There is no question that the crème de la crème of great sounding instruments originated from the hands of Strad or Guarneri. In the case of Stradivari this was recognised during his own lifetime. The perfection of craftsmanship and varnish was also unsurpassed with an extraordinarily large output. Guarneri's and Stradivari's violins have worn over the years to reveal great beauty in the layers of tones and colours in the varnish as well as the sound. The beauty of these instruments can be seen and heard with little understanding of the history, just as with a Mozart symphony.

Eduard Wulfson comments on the valuation of the instruments:

> I have respect for all my colleagues in the business, but I must say my partnerships with Christopher Reuning in Boston and Charles Beare in London unquestionably makes my team the leader on the market, which is why serious investors come to us for purchase.

There was a famous joke when a well-dressed lady came to a certain world class expert bringing a violin and asking the expert if he would be interested to look and

> sell her Stradivarius. A 1715 violin, the most important Golden Period. He said of course, by opening the case and taking out violin, the expert could see immediately it was Tirolean origin of the violin. The expert said: "What a fine Austrian Tirolean instrument." She said: "This sounds not very good to me." He said, "I apologize, it's a fine old eighteenth century Tirolean violin." She said, "No, can I suggest to you some explanation?" The expert said, "Madame, it is really around 1710–15, but Tirolean." She ventured, "What do you think about the possibility of a vacation of Stradivari in Tirol at this time?"
>
> Owners of instruments see prices going up steadily. The cheapest Strad is 5–6 million and upwards. And 22 million for del Gesù - a record for a violin, which we helped sell. That's 22 million for a cello. And two Strad violins sold for 20 million each. This amount is no longer a barrier, not a sensation, just information for the top presentable instruments, and their aura and sound and craftsmanship and period. After would be Carlo Bergonzi around 5–6 million as a confirmed price and higher to 7–8+ million. There is Amati, which would make 3–4 million, and so on. The market is always increasing.

Money is a main motivation. But so is the music. Tamio Kano from the Nippon Foundation provides a poetic explanation of an instrument to a player, and he accentuates the differences in how playing can determine the sound from the instrument:

> For a musician, an instrument is a tool to express oneself. I believe by using an instrument that is compatible with his or her skills, the musician and the instrument are brought to their best light. For many musicians, string instruments, such as violins are like a part of their body.

> The key thing about an instrument's sound is that it is not just to do with the instrument itself, but also the musician who plays it. The same instrument played by different musicians will have a different sound. Although it may not be a monetary asset, at the Nippon Music Foundation we produce recordings for every concert by our instrument loan recipients that we hold. We believe these are an important historical asset to pass on to future generations.

Suzanne Fushi recognises the importance of playing the instrument and the impact it may have on the valuation of the instrument, or, at minimum, to attract a buyer, even during coronavirus:

> Who played an instrument is of historic importance and can add value to an instrument. In many cases the quality of the instrument goes hand in hand with the person that chose it as their musical partner. Vieuxtemps chose an extraordinary Guarneri del Gesù that was one of the most expensive violins ever sold. When you think of some artists you immediately think of their unforgettable tone. The violin is definitely a partner in that endeavor.
>
> Our violins are played in concert halls throughout the world routinely, except in these strange times! We present a concert series in Chicago which began in 2006 and have nine recitals each year. We also present approximately five masterclasses each season. I look forward to when we all can begin again. Until then, we've started a program called Stradivari Society Artists In Residence. While our artists are not able to travel the world to perform due to the pandemic, they have some time to teach remotely. It's a great opportunity for emerging artists to learn from some of the best violinists of our time.

Jason Price of Tarisio Auction House considers the instrument as a work of art, not only a performance piece and shares his opinion about the playing of the instrument and its ancillary value:

> I take a slightly different approach here. Yes, instruments sound better when they are actively played but this is more a process of keeping them in shape, not improving them. On the contrary, playing an instrument is a deleterious process: no matter how careful a musician is, the act of playing an instrument inevitably creates wear and micro-damage to the instrument and increases its exposure to damage and loss. Violins must be played, this is imperative, but it's disingenuous to say that instruments get better the more they are played. I believe that 99.9999% of the world's instruments should be under chins nightly but that last fraction of a percent should be preserved so that future generations can know them like we do.

Perhaps the most passionate answer about the purchasing and playing of a rare instrument comes from Eduard Wulfson, the teacher of soloists Kristóf Baráti, Daniel Lozakovitj, Marc Bouchkov and Alexandra Conunova, and who sold the David Fulton Collection of instruments to the Mariinsky Theatre in 2016:

Wulfson was asked: If the master instruments require such a master player, how do you recognise a talent worthy of such a rare instrument? Especially if such talent can impact the value of the investment? Only the teacher can tell.

> There is the possibility to answer via nice stories which are absolutely truthful. For instance with Kristóf Baráti, it was a funny beginning. He was a sixteen-year-old boy and participated in the Paris Jacques Thibaud competition. I was invited to present a Stradivarius for

sale to a Japanese player. Out of noblesse oblige, I was obligated to listen to her. The rules were three would play in a row. And as I was invited to sit in the middle of the parterre, it would be impossible to leave. The first candidate was the Japanese to whom I was supposed to sell the violin. By all respect to my business activities, they are not always matching the talent of the player. She was disastrously bad, but I say this with a sense of humour. Then I saw and heard the Hungarian sixteen-year-old Kristóf Baráti. All candidates started with the 2nd movement of the Mozart 4th Concerto K218 Re maggiore, and the young boy made a note of absolute exception. In the first few bars, the line of musicianship, the sound production and beauty of phrase and capacity of tensions was immediately evident and allowed us to see someone exceptional, because of his desire to listen to each note without breaking into fragments. Of course, I immediately realized some matters which could be corrected to make it more professional, and sure of developing such a great talent.

To compare it to a beautiful portrait or fresco, where some of the figures make perfection. It is always my duty as pedagogue as coach to offer the knowledge. The problem is how to offer and why. The instrument was in this case the solution. Baráti played on the most awful East European violin, twentieth century, that was impossible to identify. Impressed as I was as to how he played Mozart and Wienawski, I offered him the private selection of my collection, which was a Goffriller and a Stradivarius and Guarneri, father of del Gesù. It was very funny, because he didn't know who I was. As he mentioned later, he thought I was a wealthy patron who just wanted to lend the instrument to a gifted boy, but he didn't have a clue about my other professional capacities. At the moment to decide on the instruments offered, it was the moment I informed him I had to leave for an imminent departure.

He chose the most fantastic 1690 Goffriller for comfort. He won the 2nd prize. He should have won 1st. Today, most people think the decision was a mistake.

Baráti became my student after the Paris competition. He was in shock when I showed him what he could do and what he could study. It was for preparation of the Queen Elizabeth Competition. From his point of view, I was so sophisticated as a teacher. I don't understand what means coach, teacher and mentor. For me they are all together. I was very surprised and said I hope I match your expectation. To be clear, I have stayed as his mentor and coach more than twelve years.

Regarding Lozakovitj, my beloved Daniel. Again, it was innocent, because I was invited by Martin Engström to be part of the Verbier Festival in many directions. As a sponsor, and as a deep long friend. I prepared many players to be part of the festival. And participate as both artist and artistic advisor. The concert was to be conducted by Valery Gergiev, my friend of 45 years; it was an important event because it was to be an homage to Maya Plisetskaya, to the greatest ballerina of our time, who had passed away. During the rehearsal Valery was extremely emotional, because he was a great friend of Maya and her husband, the composer Rodion Shchedrin. Everyone was moved because the immortal Plisetskaya danced *Bolero* on the screen, and the music was played by the Verbier Festival Orchestra accompanying the film, conducted by Valery. Then Tchaikovsky's *Pathetique Symphony*. This whole atmosphere was deeply moving. Meanwhile, I was contacted by Engström to block Valery's exit from the concert hall because it was arranged Valery would listen to a small boy of fourteen years old, Daniel Lozakovitj. I was asked to give my opinion as if they needed. I felt very important and flattered. He began to play the Sibelius Concerto from beginning. And my modest judgement told me that he was a great talent, probably the greatest which could be present. Again, my professional experience told me there were elements to work on and improve. But it was not difficult for me to confirm this judgement to Valery and Martin. Then it goes in a funny and interesting direction. There is some lady who came to me and asked if I could be interested to listen more deeply, because it was only five minutes. "Would it be possible to work with him?" she asked. "Is her your son?" I asked. "He is a fantastic talent." I said neither yes or no. "He's not my son," she said. "I am the daughter of the ex-president of Kyrgyzstan, but this boy is my friend's son. So I ask if you would give some lessons to him to deepen your opinion about this boy." "Yes, of course," I replied.

He or she as a teacher has to be able to make immediate progress and be responsible or is not qualified for this position to be teacher of a genius. Not in one month, not in two months, but immediately to understand, because of knowledge, talent, experience, and to make a professional communication and a decision using language and explanation to show clear examples if it is necessary on the instrument. And it was funny, it was Ravel *Tzigane*, and at the beginning you have to put the bow in the right place and from the strings you make a motion of the bow and then calculate the rhythm inside. And then with the Mozart concert and other repertoire, it was a very nice introduction. The boy was more curious about me than I was about him. For me nothing changed. The amazing talent was already there. There was another session between us in Stockholm, where he was born and lived with his parents. I went for another business appointment for Gergiev and he was conducting the Radio Orchestra of Stockholm and Mariinsky Orchestra in several concerts for the Baltic Festival. In Stockholm I continued working with Daniel, and there was a moment when the fourteen-year-old boy told me, for instance in 2nd movement of the Sibelius Concerto and other pieces we worked on, he realized the person he would like to engage to be his coach and teacher and mentor, which was designated in his own mind, would be me. My answer is when I spoke apologetically to my wife: My dear, our next vacation to Seychelles is to be postponed.

Back to the instruments I recommended to Daniel. He played a modest Grancino violin lent to him by a Scandinavian Foundation. The small boy, I say with love, told me he was promised a Stradivarius, but all the adults lied to him, but no one is seriously lending one. Ok, I told him. You will get it. He said, "I don't believe this happiness will be so easy for me to get." In Sweden, when he told me I was his coach, mentor and teacher, when he came to Geneva for the first working sessions, it was an amazing challenge for me, because he was invited to play Saint-Saëns *Havanese* and *Rondo Capriccioso*, with National de Lyon conducted by Leonard Slatkin, and also the Sibelius Concerto in Sweden. I had to prove myself otherwise Seychelles would come back. I offered him the 1712 Stradivari, *ex-Viotti*. It was lent by me and Chris Reuning. Not hard to convince Reuning when he heard Daniel play. Daniel understood how difficult it was to play these instruments. He began to work harder to get the Maitrise d'instrument. As the story goes deeper, the Saint-Saëns was very successful. Also the Sibelius. Fortunately, I was not fired and it was the right decision from my wife's point of view.

To be precise, these instruments are difficult, extremely sophisticated instruments. To arrive to sound and spirit of composer into the sound, it is extremely difficult combination of requested matters. We have experience to listen to those instruments when Heifetz played his del Gesù or Menuhin *Lord Wilton* or his Strad in possession of Perlman, or Francescatti, or Henryk

> Szeryng or Milstein, we hear the effort to match their genius abilities to match the instruments capabilities. So from that point of view, Daniel immediately realized the possibility for him to deepen his mastership. Then after use of the instruments for more than two years, we decided to go for the better one, what that means is the one more suitable for him. The 1713 *ex-Rothschild*. This violin was lent by Reuning and myself, after his Boston Symphony debut in Tanglewood, when the still small boy, played marvellously Sol Maggiore Concert K216 from Mozart on the *ex-Viotti*." Then he switched to the *ex-Rothschild* for the Tchaikovsky Concerto with hr-Sinfonieorchester Frankfurt, and for Beethoven with Mariinsky and Gergiev.
>
> I have been his teacher for five years. And I am still not fired. It is such a sophisticated and hard work that drives us to understand the technological levels of virtuosity to the Mt. Everest top of achievement. Because the music that requests to be played, Beethoven, Tchaikovsky, Prokofiev 2, Bach Concerti, all he recorded for Deutsche Grammophon. Yes, it feels good not to be fired. Either you're the top and not fired or not matching the expectations and fired. But these geniuses need to be served with the best.

David Fulton's collection, considered the best in the world in its prime in the early 2000s, is a prime example of asset appreciation. Fulton began collecting in 1981, after purchasing a Guarneri violin. Instead of becoming a musician, he pursued the study of mathematics and eventually founded Fox Software, which he sold to Microsoft in 1992. Fulton retired in 1994, and he and his wife devoted their immense wealth and passion to building their collection of rare instruments and sponsoring world-class musicians and local arts organisations through what is known as the David and Amy Fulton Foundation. Fulton then decided to reduce his collection of twenty-two instruments down to the fifteen of the most exceptional master instruments, nine violins, three violas and three cellos, including a priceless collection of bows. Fulton said to the *Financial Times* in a 2009 article: "There was nowhere to go… The *Lord Wilton* is the finest del Gesù instrument and *La Pucelle* is the finest Strad, short of the *Messiah*.'" Where did he go? To Russia with Love.

Eduard Wulfson, with Christopher Reuning and Charles Beare, made the sale of a lifetime. Valery Gergiev, arguably the most powerful and highest paid conductor in the world, as Music Director of the Munich Philharmonic and Artistic and General Director of the Mariinsky Theatre in St. Petersburg, purchased, with the support of the Kremlin, the Fulton Collection to create something extraordinary: the Mariinsky Stradivarius Ensemble. The Mariinsky Stradivarius Ensemble is a group of musicians "who perform on the world's most famous and unique-sounding string instruments in the world." It includes the finest instrumentalists and lead soloists in the Mariinsky Orchestra. The repertoire takes on a new sound and focus due to the incredibly rich and beautiful timbres of the instruments of Amati, Stradivari, Guarneri, Guadagnini and Goffriller.

Wulfson describes the moment of the sale:

> Regarding other aspects, in the history of institutions, such great European and American orchestras always have the need for great instruments for the soloists because of the repertoire. And patrons and conductors, of repertoire with solo violin, like Strauss and Rimsky-Korsakov, Brahms, etc… there is always need for good instruments.
>
> All major orchestras had patrons who provided the money to purchase the instruments. If a wealthy family or institution would acquire or purchase, they would contribute. The San Francisco Symphony, Los Angeles Philharmonic have Strads, New York Philharmonic and Boston Symphony and Concertgebouw, Berlin Phil…. My point of view is the institutional relationship came later. It was the period of the twentieth century when wealthy

countries, like the USA after the war, kept a tradition to provide to soloist an instrument, to get at least good instruments in the group – Guadagnini, Gagliano, etc…

Then came the 1989 explosion of the Soviet Empire. They had a state collection of instruments but built it in a dishonest way, as an appropriation from aristocrats. So it was badly managed and the instruments never got played. We have to be careful in post-Soviet time – many musicians came to US and Israel and Europe. Still there was a tradition of two major opera houses, Bolshoi and Mariinsky (formerly known as the Kirov).

The Mariinsky was led by Yuri Temirkanov who left to lead the Leningrad Philharmonic Orchestra, which then became the St. Petersburg Philharmonic. Then Gergiev comes to Mariinsky. Valery does an incredible job and creates all this energy with a phenomenal workaholic ability to motivate the theatre. At that time it was only famous for ballet. He makes another level increasing more activity for the orchestra, chorus, opera and ballet. Better than the Bolshoi which was still struggling with intrigues. Gergiev arranged serious sponsors and a good relationship with the government to get unconditional support for his institution. It was still Yeltsin time. But in the fastest time he created repertoire, an all-Russian repertoire, so the orchestra could be so virtuosic that they could come to any concert stage and opera house. On a world class level. Renaissance par excellence. Gergiev had the idea, because he guest conducts all the greatest orchestras in the world, he sees and hears the quality of instruments played – when he conducts *Scheherazade*, he sees the disadvantages in his own orchestra. So 2008–09, he sees the fall of the rouble. It was an opportunity at that time to rebuild his orchestra in the name of Russia. To convince the government that it is a good idea. Many dealers like flies jumped to the first plane to Saint Petersburg from London to NYC to propose him instruments. I got a call from Valery – he wants to meet. "Of course, I always go to your concerts." "No, don't bullshit," said Gergiev, "you know what I mean. Our meeting is in London tomorrow." After a rehearsal with the LSO, we go to dinner with friends. After dinner, We have three hours to walk from the National Gallery through Trafalgar Square. Gergiev likes to talk during motion. I needed to talk because of the tense conversation. I said, "Look, you know me, and you found out I am a leader on the market. I would advise you to have the best; I never sign contract. A handshake is more important." "You are my advisor," he said. I said, "Be careful."

I found the Guarneri cello, then I found other beautiful instruments, the Fulton collection which was offered via Charles Beare, a 42 million deal, six instruments. With Valery, he is a good friend, but I have privileges... *King Joseph* del Gesù 1737, Montagnana cello 1737, Stradivari 1733 *Sassoon*, so many. I told him: "Take it or leave it. Dr. Fulton is not willing to wait months until somebody would give a word." So here I am, frustrated in Vienna in the Imperial Hotel. Gergiev was very busy conducting everywhere. It was difficult to get through, because so many people have to go through him to make negotiations. I see the cleaning lady – I said open the door. She did it because I was so clear to her, despite it being illegal. I came into the room, the suite of Valery. I knocked on his suite, and he came out of the bath, unshaved, with a lot of mousse. "Oh, Eduard, if you jump in the room in this way, then it must be important." I said, "The Fulton collection is for sale." He stopped immediately. He was very concentrated. "Give me five minutes," he said. "You have it," I answered. He came out and said, "I am sure deal is on the table. Please start to make arrangements." Of course it was a long negotiation and many things happened after. Contracts, expectations, etc. but we succeeded. Valery is a leader in

> the musical world because he is not giving a life plan to the purchase. He has a Plan B for beautiful instruments to also play and improve the quality of the orchestra. Unique investments. The Fulton Collection was bought completely. People know Gergiev is the biggest collector now, but because of need not only because of the desire to own. The sound of the orchestra is better. The need was fulfilled.

The need is not always fulfilled. While Wulfson, Reuning and Beare were able to engineer the ideal sale for authenticated rare instruments now owned, played and preserved by the Mariinsky Theatre and its Stradivarius Ensemble, some instances when such international sales were fabricated have created chaos and criminals in the process. As the saying goes: Buyers beware.

## *Investor Challenges: Dealer Trafficking and Fraud*

Dietmar Machold, once known as "Mr. Stradivarius," was among the world's most influential dealers in rare instruments. He admitted he embezzled money made from the sale of instruments entrusted to him by his clients and customers, but denied fraud charges as his 2010 trial got under way in Vienna.

He was a flamboyant charlatan, therefore, able to fool others. He socialised in high society and even lived in an Austrian castle. He bragged about a garage full of expensive cars and he collected luxury watches and cameras. Indeed, his reputation as a global dealer of rare instruments, just as China and Korea emerged as the next big markets, demonstrating both interest and purchasing power, allowed him to move in and out of the highest circles of music and money.

He had dealerships in Zürich, Vienna, New York and Chicago, serving soloists and collectors. It seemed all was ideal, but with such fame and fortune come many risks. Being addicted to power exposed his temptations and weaknesses. The entire empire collapsed in 2010 into bankruptcy and multimillion dollar lawsuits.

"This ascent was built on sand," said Herbert Harammer, the prosecutor of the trial against Machold told the court, accusing Machold of leading a lifestyle that was a facade for a business that had actually been insolvent for nearly five years.

Machold claimed innocence and denied charges of fraud, but he did acknowledge diverting five rare instruments entrusted to him for sale by clients, including a Stradivarius violin from 1727, that court documents valued at around €2.6 million.

"All these (instruments) were used illegally. I confess fully," Machold told the court, saying he was in desperate need of money. Machold's castle 'Eichbeuchl" was at risk of being foreclosed, and he hid his cars, camera and watch collection from creditors. He accumulated debts of €250 million.

Machold lied to other dealers, investors and collectors and overvalued worthless instruments, such as a cello he said was worth $300,000 but which the prosecutor said could be bought on eBay for less than $2000.

Florian Leonhard worked with Machold. He says:

> Machold stylized himself into something he wasn't. He wanted to be number one. The way to be number one is to be an expert, which he was not, neither a maker nor an expert. In order to gain momentum. I would like you to have a magnifying glass on all the people. Whether they are really experts or building image. Experts are few in a generation. There is a reason. It is not that many people are not capable of that, many have more than me, but not the right makeup inside yourself and the right situation.
>
> You want to be a violin maker, to be in one of the best shops in the world, and it was the opportunity in my lifetime to absorb how different schools worked. I came from an art background; my father a painter. It wasn't imposed on me. It was my interest. I don't even know

who gave me the interest to find out why this school not that school. It was a psychological and sociological thing. I was trying to understand schools of thought. In painters you could see Venetian school or Florentine or sixteenth [century]. Because of different political circumstances created a different need for creations, plus craft that was local. Same thing for violin making based on certain circumstances.

In Cremona it was a unique situation, coming out of Amati. His success was able to take these Renaissance principles to interest the king of Spain to order an orchestra of instruments; He had pupils to help make them to create the school which became Stradivari and Guarneri. At the beginning you don't understand it and you try to make a map. It took me fifteen years to put the puzzle together. It's a lifetime passion and time involvement and not something you can put on your shirt. I am an expert. And the person who is consulted by those who call themselves experts. I can see the level of interest. I also don't like how many violin makers only see themselves. I love to share in a great world. Because the violin dealing world, if you're not fully in it yourself, you may not understand.

Machold had a chance. Why not say anything? You could not say anything because in our market, even with some people today because people are so scared to buy from a dealer because someone could play that game.

People come to me and before the purchase I will make a full investigation. I will go on my detective search. People call me "The Sherlock Holmes of the violin world." I have to see every piece of paper and stylistically analyse is it the same, any alteration, is varnish the same, all from same violin, is the scroll fitting. So many parameters to make the search. And I take enormous pride in this. Machold did it wrong. I want to remain true to myself and others.

Wulfson went on about Machold and other noted examples of rare instrument fraud:

> Goldman Sachs was supposed to be the money behind a Beijing Orchestra invented by Machold. He just needed instruments to sell to somebody else and then hide the money. At that time, there were some Taiwanese, Japanese collectors. But it was all criminal what he did.
>
> Dealing with Machold, it was my first and last time. There was a violin that Salvatore Accardo owned. My dealing was always as a friend and business partner, and I bought shares in the instrument and then sold as common property, despite being a minority owner. It was the Stradivarius *Firebird* 1718 violin. We had interesting prospects to sell in Finland and Switzerland, then in a weird and crooked way, there was another scandal that was a settlement case with Peter Biddulph, a court case, and he was in trouble, and at that time, I was too weak to resist. When you're younger, you wish to have a finger in every deal. Rumours started to spread about Machold, his dealing and not paying on time, and Machold would go to prison if he did anything criminal. Of course, I soon found out the violin was sold in Salt Lake City but Machold pretended he bought it himself. I called Machold, and told him: "You sold the violin that you pretended to buy, but you didn't pay me. I give you two weeks, time is ticking, and my oral conversation would be followed by the lawyer letter confirming my statement to you." Funny story was I was getting a call from an Austrian bank, also corrupt, and they said they are holding money for the *Firebird* violin. Mr. Machold said this money should be paid in your account. I confirmed and I agreed warmly their transfer abilities. Seemed the reason for the calling is they didn't trust their client. They replied: "No, we always call the receiver when important transfers." The only thing that pleased me in

this situation after I received the money is that someone will confirm. The money arrived next day after the call by SWIFT, then I was enjoying myself by telling the bank I changed my mind after I got the money! Then after that I advised all my colleagues and dealers and experts like Reuning, Beare, and others to stop dealings and make barriers with Machold. Unfortunately, one of the buyers did not follow my advice and was misused and violated by this criminal Machold who invented the story about the creation of a Chinese orchestra in Beijing which would be backed by Goldman Sachs and they would buy ten violins, five celli and five viola, which was all bullshit.

Unfortunately, people gave him instruments to make the deal. When the instruments were sold to other parties it was difficult to trace them. Then he never paid the Ponzi scheme, like four or five deals in the back. Then he was arrested. I was advising a friend but never acted as a witness. Problem was the international victims. If it was an international court it would be better to do then according to Austrian legislation. Machold is one of biggest crooks in the history of crime, not only with respect to rare instruments.

My company would not make statements about the trust, and my records and ethical and professional responsibility would give a guarantee to the next owner. This is the difference between writing a certificate in our opinion, but the guarantee to stay behind the bill, because of our financial strength and Swiss law which would be an extra guarantee, because in Switzerland, registered in the chamber of commerce in Geneva, any fraudulent and negligent actions would not be tolerated by Swiss legal thinking. We make all due diligence in making the deal. Clear relationships to the ex-owners. And if my company owns or consigns, it's impossible to have the condition of the instrument in doubt in such a professional atmosphere, which I create as a leader

> on the market. The only explanation would be greed, negligence and dead professional judgement or criminal background which could be explained for this kind of fraud. In violin dealing, every thirty years, there are frauds and disastrous situations which could be easily avoided if they would not be negligent, greedy, stupid people. We make the due diligence. We observe many transactions that would not be approved in our time. It is nothing personal but it is professional because of many instruments sold which could be questionable. I would never interfere in the criminal selling to a criminal. How many are on the market anyway?

A scandal every thirty years? Known as "The Flying Fiddle," among industry elites, the Biddulph scandal, referred to by Wulfson, brought Peter Biddulph to the edge of bankruptcy. He was taken to court by a wealthy widower named Vera Farnsworth, whose partner Gerald Segelman had collected several rare instruments and now, after his passing, needed to be sold. Biddulph was accused of being a dishonest agent in handling Segelman's legacy, including three Stradivarius instruments estimated to be worth more than $1.25 million each. Biddulph was deliberately undervaluing violins and secretly pocketing the difference. In the settlement, Biddulph paid £3 million to the executors of Segelman's will, nearly wiping out his business. Fortunately, Peter Biddulph has returned to solvency and success. Lessons were learned for both dealer and collector to be scrupulous and sincere.

In some cases, that judgement can be dangerous. Herbert Axelrod (everyone assumes we are related, and we did meet years before his passing and tried to determine the family connection to no avail), an ichthyologist and pet-care multimillionaire who invested in rare instruments from the money made from his pre-internet publishing business, was arrested in 2004 for tax reasons unrelated to his violin investment scheme to sell part of his vast collection of instruments to the New Jersey Symphony

Orchestra. The names of Axelrod and his wife Evelyn were also engraved on the concert hall entrance as patrons for the New Jersey Performing Arts Center in Newark. Axelrod was one of the few people to actually sell violins to an orchestra with the intention to upgrade the quality and sound of his hometown orchestra. That deal was historic in dimensions. After a year of wrangling with Axelrod, the orchestra wound up borrowing $18 million, including $4 million from Axelrod himself, to buy what it dubbed "The Golden Age Collection." Among the twenty-four violins, two violas and four cellos are twelve instruments credited to Antonio Stradivari and two to Guarneri del Gesù.

Mr. Axelrod then forgave $1 million and later donated $2.1 million toward the purchase. After initial estimates were released that said the collection was worth a whopping $50 million, the orchestra demanded an internal review and its own appraisers put the worth at $15.3 million to $26.4 million. A $24 million-plus difference tax penalty to pay. Who was right? Axelrod refused to admit any wrongdoing and did what most people did back in the old days. He fled to Switzerland. There he became one of the largest patrons of the Zürich Opera and Tonhalle Orchestra. But there he was also caught, arrested in Berlin, for tax evasion for a matter unrelated to the instrument IRS bill.

As noted in a 2007 article by Daniel Wakin in the *New York Times*, Herbert Axelrod had overstayed the value of the thirty instruments, which included Guarneri and Stradivarius. The red flag also put the orchestra into deep debt. To reduce the debt, two twin brother investors, Brook and Seth Taube, paid $20 million and some of the profits from future sales of the instruments, and they kept two Strads one from 1701 and one from 1710. The orchestra continued to play these instruments for another five years and eventually came out of debt in 2011, and the investors became instant collectors. Axelrod passed away in 2017. His wife Evelyn still acts as the trustee of the Evelyn and Herbert Axelrod Stiftung in Zürich continuing their support of the arts. All's well that ends well.

Sometimes, however, it is not even the under or over valuation. It might even be a fake instrument. It is a subject as important as it is in art. Counterfeit or fake instruments do exist and are regularly sold on the market. There are many falsely labelled Stradivarius instruments sold and bought and even played by soloists who promote them as a real Stradivarius. I personally know of a certain soloist in Switzerland who promotes her violin as a 1732 Stradivarius. The proof? The label inside. And a photo from an old book which suggests image similarity. Any dendrology? Nope. Any appraisals? Nada. Yet the media do not do their research. They are happy to write about a violinist with a Strad because it might increase readership, whether it is verified or not. And the soloist will not complain. Do the dealers and collectors? Perhaps they should.

Nigel Brown offers some advice:

> I think it's very difficult to carry off a fake in this world. Because fakes don't work. Just because someone has a violin with a label that says Strad doesn't make it one. The sound it produces is not commensurate with the sound in my ear of what a Strad sounds like. Depending on the player and circumstances, the fake will be shown up loud and clear. If it was played in Wigmore Hall it would be detected. I'd be sitting there and saying this person needs another violin. One has to be cautious. I've never called them out. It would take chutzpah. It's not necessarily my place to tell people that they are misrepresenting the violin.

Suzanne Fushi is more stoic about the frequency of such fake instruments saturating the market:

> It is an important subject. I can't even guess how many fake Strads are out there. They have labels that have given false hope to many. We get photos of them regularly. We do our own appraisals.

Jason Price considers the codification and authentication of instruments to be vital to their survival:

> There is a rich history of counterfeits and swindles in the violin business but luckily most of this is in the past. Tarisio does all its own internal expertise but what makes us unique in this business is that we guarantee our attributions against that of our contemporaries. If we say a violin is a Grancino this means that we are willing to submit that opinion to the review of our peers, in fact we encourage it, and this routs out any "outlier attributions," making the transaction safer for the purchaser. Furthermore Tarisio has fully embraced the technological tools that have added a forensic basis to expertise over the past 30 years: dendrochronology, CT scanning, metal spectrology and the general sharing of information like with our Cozio Archive project.

Wulfson as a pedagogue and dealer has much more to say on the subject:

> What makes one year better than another? The concentration of genius is in Stradiivari himself. There is the presence of his sons – all good luthiers, but missing the genius of the father. Expensive because of name, but not the same aura and sound and craft as Antonio would craft himself. Some exceptions do exist. Some participation of Bergonzi, but mainly Antonio's sound concept was there.
>
> Soloists claim to play a Stradivarius to be famous because the playing is not good enough. People who try to sell an instrument can make mistakes from the temptations to have money or not to have money. There are different ways. If it is not successful it is not meant to be. I had an experience with Reuning in Boston, selling a Stradivari cello. Three persons showed enormous interest to purchase. One was very wealthy Asian client

> from Taiwan. It was funny the idea that I should bring the cello to him for approval to take pay of purchase. I saw myself in the mirror, if someone would like to insult me, I could react, take personally or not pay attention. Normally unpleasant, but why should some kind of wealthy man, would insult the most perfect Stradivari cello, by asking for an examination in Taipei. "You would fly 1st class private jet," he said. I could afford that, no problem. But no doubt I will not do that, because it will be an insult to one of the greatest examples of art and craftsmanship on earth. Why not the buyer come to see the cello and buy? Finally, there was a private jet, but from some other customer who came to me and so I opened the case. I was offered $14 million for the cello. The person asked to negotiate. My handshake is the negotiation. There are no negotiations. We make a handshake and meet for the deal. Lawyers were together and deal was done. There is some dignity that should be applied. If you respect a great collector or maestro, then you have to make an effort to make it possible. Because one is a billionaire does not qualify him enough to make the examination. The next Stradivari cello would be $25–26 million, the $14 million would be a huge profit. There are a few elements which always make the same story. This puzzle to resolve and to find out answers are simple. Professionalism, ethics, honesty, and all other aspects come together to make a deal. The right conditions and the right moment are 100% reassurance.

Investors should know that string instruments with fake labels and even bogus attributions are far greater than the genuine thing. Just because the instrument has a Stradivarius label inside does not mean it is the real McCoy. Given the reputation of Stradivarius, Amati and Guaneri, by the late nineteenth century, many German and French violin makers added a fake label to increase sales. Many clients purchased these violins, thinking them to be genuine, only to learn later they were not. This led to the McKinley Tariff Act of 1890, forcing manufacturers to put the place of origin on their labels. So, naturally, if you can see that a violin label reads *Antonius Stradivarius Faciebat Anno 1723, made in Germany*, the answer is obvious, it was made after 1890. Even If the label doesn't have the place of origin, it most likely is not a real Strad violin if it has no provenance or papers. In short, most violins with a Stradivari label are copies and can be proven thanks to the technology available today. That adds some comfort to the interested investor.

Christopher Marinello says:

> With today's technology, we have seen incredible fakes and forgeries produced that can fool many so-called experts. Fortunately, technology is a double-edged sword and we work with some top forensic laboratories to uncover fake art and instruments that are offered for sale in the marketplace. When we find a stolen object being offered for sale, we always confirm that it is, in fact, the same object that was stolen. Sometimes that requires the assistance of a specialist lab but in most cases, we have enough on file to confirm the match.

Jonathan Moulds talks about the advances in technology not only for authenticity but performance as well.

> You go back 150 years, there are not that many violinists that stand out. The number of soloists that have any real impact short term on an instrument are minimal. Like Perlman, but it would have to be a great instrument. It is mainly the instrument that justifies the value. Over longer term, a soloist of particular renown could help. For me it makes a difference. Up and coming soloist and can make the most out of the instrument. I don't loan the instrument because I think it will go up in value because XYZ played it.

> How would technology make a difference in the value of the artist? Mutter, Kavakos, Vengerov, it might help the instrument increase, but they don't agree on any one instrument. It is a broader question as to what the soloist likes. These are instruments made 300 years ago, and that is more illustrative of a trend that something is being played over such a time frame, more than any one artist. There are specializations. What fits somebody well, doesn't mean physically fit another well. And yet, it doesn't make a difference on the underlying value.

Should the investor make a separate appraisal once the instrument is offered for sale to determine its authenticity, especially at auction, or is it better work exclusively with dealers who provide this authenticity?

As one of the most respected collectors in the world. Jonathan Moulds speaks volumes to the interested investor who might fear such forgeries.

> I work only with dealers and dealers that I trust. The evolution of science and technology can be very beneficial here. To me, the most important issue to consider in buying an instrument is the expertise of the dealer and their ability to provide relevant perspective. Most rare instruments have a history, often detailed, and multiple records do exist in many cases. Not all dealers have access to such records and I think the more relevant information a potential purchaser can see the better.

Bruno Price and Ziv Arazi share a very important point about damage to an instrument: Repairing can be worse than the challenges of recovery.

> Sadly one doesn't need license to work on violins and there are many tragic stories of repairmen doing unnecessary work with little or no regard to preservation. There is one

> infamous maker who is still active today who has devalued several of the greatest instruments due to his excessive and invasive repair techniques. In the past these incidents were kept quiet, usually because the owners were embarrassed to have trusted this person and knew that suing was not an option as he had no insurance and no money. So through a lot of PR from musician friends who don't know better, these vandals continue working today.

If you are an investor, how would you protect the investment? Insurance policies are the norm of the industry but how much are they? Are there other ways to ensure the protection required? What about strict guidelines by the owner or investor who lends the instrument? Who pays for the insurance? The owner or the soloist who is given the instrument to play? Does that matter in the case of recovery?

Christopher Marinello works with insurance companies in the valuation and recovery of rare instruments. Just as an investor would buy insurance for a car or home, an antique rare instrument requires specialised policies and coverage.

> Insurance from a specialist fine art or instrument insurer is very important when you acquire a valuable instrument. Updating your insurance schedule annually is also important since most rare instruments increase in value over the years. I can't tell you how many underinsured objects I see get stolen only to find that the owners never updated their policies. They discover this when they get paid a fraction of what the object is actually worth or what it would cost to replace. The strict guidelines that insurers place on art and musical instruments serve to protect the insurance company. However, these guidelines are not impossible to live with otherwise museums would not lend works of art to other museums. My advice is to know what your policy says and take advice from a lawyer if necessary before you lend an instrument. Follow the policy

> guidelines to the letter which might include obtaining permission from the Underwriter. When an instrument is stolen and the victim is paid out, the object becomes the property of the insurer when it is recovered. This is called subrogation. Know your rights under the policy. With some of the better Insurers, you can repay the Insurer and recover your instrument if the policy allows it.

Jason Price outlines the insurance coverage for the instruments on auction:

> Insurance covers nearly all exposures for musical instruments. Most policies provide exclusions for acts of war and for leaving musical instruments unattended in a motor vehicle, but other than that, damage, loss and theft are insurable risks.

Christopher Marinello is on the front line of recovery and lays out the process and timeline:

> These are very important steps to get right and do early.
>
> 1. Notify the police and get a police report number or case number, even if "lost in transit." I will need this number to recover the instrument when it resurfaces. Keep all paperwork.
> 2. Contact your Insurer. Report the loss, the circumstances, and provide them with all photographs/receipts that you have been keeping all these years.
> 3. Register the loss on international databases such as the non-profit Artive Database (www.artive.org) or the FBI, Carabinieri, Interpol databases depending on where the theft occurred.
> 4. Contact me at Art Recovery International if you have any problems or issues with the above.

I am always happy to help victims of crime and guide them through the process needed to file reports to the right people.

Generally speaking, when a stolen instrument is located somewhere for sale or when it has been brought in for repair, the first step is usually to determine whether it was a recent theft with an open criminal investigation or an old crime where the police may be less interested. We always give the police an opportunity to get involved in the recovery or take it over if they wish. In most cases, they let us do the work and only ask to be kept informed. If the police don't think they can get an arrest, they are usually not very interested. We then confront the person selling or in possession of the stolen instrument and demand their documentation. They usually demand the same from us and we present them with that all important documentation I mentioned earlier. Police report, crime reference number, purchase and insurance documentation (usually redacted by me to protect the victim's privacy). I then explain the law to the possessor or their lawyer and negotiate a return of the object or reach a negotiated settlement depending on the strength of the case, the laws in the jurisdiction we are operating in, and the wishes of the victim or their family. If I don't get cooperation from the possessor, I can usually count on law enforcement to back me up which goes back to why I want thefts reported to the police.

I work with a number of brilliant provenance researchers all over the world who know their way around historic archives and obtain the documentation we need to launch a successful recovery. These researchers can spot a falsified provenance and know the "red flag names" that require extra scrutiny. We often come across cases where the original theft victim or the heirs have had a hand in the "theft." Sometimes, this rises to the level of insurance fraud. We do our best to resolve such delicate issues amicably and without the need for court intervention.

Most people, when confronted, choose to cooperate.

Much has been written about the Nazi plunder of fine art, but few efforts to analyse their confiscation of musical treasures have been made. Now researchers are beginning to focus on the issue, and at the University of California's Institute of European Studies in Berkeley, there is a project on musical losses, file by file, name by name. The analysis of authenticity and the history of ownership and possession, the provenance, are essential to the mission.

Marinello is clear:

> When we are researching stolen or Nazi-looted works of art, an object's provenance plays a great part in any potential recovery. This would apply to instruments and manuscripts as well.

And yet, there are many for which provenance could not prevail. Marinello's work remains an "unfinished symphony." Take note of the following outstanding mysteries. Once they do surface, which most think they will, the sale may break new records. Investors be ready!

Where is the violin listed in Viennese records as an "Antonius Stradivarius Cremonensis faciebat Anno 1722," confiscated in 1939 from the noted art collector Oskar Bondy?

Or two violins that had belonged to the Austrian composer Johann Strauss II, seized from his Jewish stepdaughter?

Did Josef Goebbels give away a stolen violin, or has the violinist Nejiko Suwa who received it been unfairly tainted for decades by the stain of Nazism?

During the war, a Nazi intelligence unit called the Sonderstab Musik was responsible for confiscating the musical manuscripts, printed music, books and, as one would expect, rare instruments. Art Recovery International and other researchers seek out certifications of authenticity, appraisals, bills of sale, photographs, ledgers, letters and diaries to restore the instruments to the rightful owners or heirs.

However, the provenance for these instruments that show up in auctions or dealer's showrooms is usually limited, sometimes forged, and sometimes simply do not exist. Trade customs intended to protect legitimate privacy interests of owners nonetheless frustrate efforts to trace instruments that may have been illegally taken by the Third Reich. Owner's names are often erased on privacy grounds and given terms like "from the collection of a professional musician."

Christopher Marinello believes it is necessary to recover these instruments which are both personal treasures and cultural relics of national identity. Even if there has not been a major *New York Times* headline of a stolen Strad, ignoring the problem only makes the investment a potential liability, not to mention an ethically challenging conundrum.

Forget the label printed inside the violin's left f-hole. The process of authenticating the instrument can be as detailed and minute as brain surgery. Dendrochronology tests on the wood may provide not only the date but even the geographic location. The varnish and its application, notwithstanding the use of blood, might also be a clue to the creator. An investor would be wise to have an expert like Florian Leonhard, or others interviewed in this chapter, to examine the details of craftsmanship, the style, the length of neck, and any other idiosyncrasies that would reveal the identity. Markings can be clues unlocking the mystery. The cutting of the f-holes into the belly of the violin, or the use of the Fibonacci Golden Ratio in the proportions of specific parts of the violin could make a miracle out of an instrument. Stradivari followed this mathematical equation in the measuring of the neck, pegbox and scroll to the body of the violin (upper bout, waist and lower bout) in order to result in the ratio. Also, subdivisions of the instrument – waist to upper bout, waist and upper bout to those sections plus the neck – meet the 1.6 ratio as well. However, this applies only to violins, not other string instruments, perhaps due to size.

Could this be the secret to the Stradivari? That this genius artist could recreate the divine creation of nature, of a Nautilus or a flower, and genuinely make the voice of God become sound with the stroke of bow to string?

To own a Stradivarius, a Guarneri, or an Amati might allow an owner to have a seat among the angels, in the Musica Celestis. So much of human life is spent pursuing the hope of salvation and heavenly reward. Is there another way? Could owning an instrument guarantee that which only heaven can bestow? Immortality?

***"Instruments are the bridge between the evanescent and the immortal."***
***-Jason Price, Tarisio***

A rare instrument offers an investor the opportunity to do more than see a return on the investment. It offers the investor to be a part of history. I asked each person interviewed if they consider themselves a patron, a custodian or an owner, and what immortality means to them. The answers are revealing, revelatory, and rewarding to read.

The dealers who hold a violin in their hands, express sincere humility before the mortal maker and the immortal timelessness of the instrument he made. What is important to remember is the purchase of a violin for collection or investment is as much about passion as profit, which not many people can say about a stock or a bond.

Suzanne Fushi remembers Mary Galvin, the founder of the Stradivari Society, and her father, Geoffrey Fushi. Her words reveal how such patronage creates a legacy living in memory beyond a lifetime:

> Immortality is of the utmost importance. I think of art, music, violins and their creators. I believe that in our work the past and future are always present. We preserve the past as well as possible and look to the future by supporting developing and established artists. I think of the work of my late father Geoffrey Fushi who co-

founded The Stradivari Society and believe this is a continuation of his spirit, his life's work.

I have known and worked with our founder Mary Galvin for over thirty years. We share the same mission. Our goal is to help brilliant young artists by providing the use of the best instruments possible. Mrs. Galvin has presented artists to important organizations and conductors over the years to assist with professional development. I can imagine what she's made possible throughout the years. Your question makes me think of audiences: how many people have enjoyed the recordings and concerts of young Midori with the *David* Guarneri del Gesù, or young Vadim Repin with the *Ruby* Stradivari of 1708 which is now in the phenomenal hands of Philippe Quint who goes on to perform and record on that violin; the *Auer* Stradivari with Vadim Gluzman. These are just a few examples, but there are so many more! Musicians have told me that they learned a lot about sound production from using a violin with very few limitations. One described it as being like an artist with only primary colours and then receiving a giant box of crayons with so many more colours when they received a loan from us. It is gratifying to hear how helpful and important the instruments are to the musicians.

Jonathan Moulds focuses more on the pleasure of collecting:

The only comment I would make is that as a mathematical student at Cambridge I learned to focus on the things that are tangibly possible. Just like in mathematics where there are numerous infinities, there are I suppose various variations of immortality – from physical immortality to spiritual immortality and maybe many others. In the world we live in today. I fear many people take the view that is it is worth taking the risk to die to achieve it. I am not one of those.

Simon Morris believes the immortality is only in the instruments themselves:

> Mortality is far more important to me than immortality, given that the former is guaranteed and the latter isn't. These instruments far outlive us and so one can only view it as being custodian. They have the chance to be immortal – we don't.

Florian Leonhard shares a more personal credo:

> I refer to Patek Phillipe. On the ads in the Geneva or Zurich airport, they say the same thing about owning a rare violin. You are merely the custodian of this. I feel like that. I did my skills best to help this violin to survive many more generations to come. I have goosebumps as I say this. It is an amazing feeling to be involved with something like this. Like *The Red Violin*, 300 years ago it was made, played, transported and shipped and on planes, and like a baby for people. I am passionate about this. Thats what got me into it. I will die with it. I am just somebody to facilitate that these instruments will be catalogued, secured and owned by someone.

Virginia Villa takes the perspective of preservation as the potential for immortality:

> A very difficult question. I think we can think of musical instruments, especially about violins, because that is my personal field. So, we have to remember that all these instruments are not immortal in material – wood and other materials are finite. The most important instruments now that are the most important for us, Scuola Cremonese, are 200–300 years old. Probably we don't how many years – because we don't know, it's difficult to speak about the immortality of material.

The sound we cannot also say immortal, because which sound? We must be precise – we cannot speak about immortality. We can contribute a life very long. We have received these masterpieces. And we must conserve them for history.

The intangible heritage versus tangible. In Cremona, what is recognized by UNESCO is intangible. Not just some instruments, but all the history, the first to the current makers living in Cremona, also the town. We can speak of immortality in intangible heritage.

Jason Price is inspired by the intangibility and immortality of the Stradivarius:

Sound is a short-lived beauty: produced, transmitted and then vanishing all in a fraction of a second. But the experience of music lingers a lifetime.

Instruments are the bridge between the evanescent and the immortal. I consider myself a custodian. I won't be here forever but I can leave my mark on future generations of players and collectors and makers and restorers.

Chris Marinello tends to believe the musicians are the path to preservation:

I see where you were going with that question. Yes, of course there are collectors who acquire important/rare instruments to be part of the provenance with the hope that the instrument will be known as the "(insert hedge fund billionaire here__________) Stradivarius" This happens in the art world as well with mega collectors creating small "vanity museums" around the country. While I see this as vulgar and narcissistic, I don't mind if the instruments are purchased for this reason if they are then lent out to musicians who will actually play them. With arts programs being cut worldwide, any source of funding that will benefit musicians is welcome even if it comes with a vanity plate.

Tamio Kano believes the immortality is in the continuation of custodianship:

All things have a lifespan. I believe that is true also for top quality stringed instruments such as Stradivarius. The instruments we own are those that have been kept with great care over many years by musicians, collectors, instrument dealers and organizations such as ours, which has allowed many of them to retain a close to original condition. Our mission is to pass these instruments to the next generation while continuing to maintain these instrument's wellbeing. I do not think an instrument's existence is eternal, but that is even more reason why I believe it is our mission to pass these instruments to the next generations as far as possible. We would like to continue our efforts to achieve this along with the help of musicians and instrument dealers, luthiers alike.

Nigel Brown has a more down to earth intention:

I gave up the idea I was immortal. All boys are immortal until having discovered I was not. I do feel I am part of a baton that has to be passed on and kept going. The musical baton. I'm speaking of music really, to focus on the violin, my perception was when I first got into this business. Most musicians and good players own 18th c. Italian violins. Fewer and fewer in this country. The sound quality has gotten less and less. You hear the sound quality from continental orchestras with fantastic instruments. I think in the UK most people are unaware. It never occurs to them what the instruments are, where they come from. So that was my starting point.

I'm trying to raise money here on the UK, so I'm bound to be focused on British based artists because it's easier for the people I'm talking to see the people playing. I'm very flexible, I can modify my terms if the right person. As long as I like them.

I'm not very judgmental but I have to see the person play, how they play. If they are not musical enough in my opinion, then I won't subscribe and we move on. There are lots of people I could help at various levels, I don't need to waste time on people who are not worth it. I have to believe in them. It's part of the magic. Long may it continue.

Bruno Price and Ziv Arazi wax poetic about music and time:

The great patrons who bought instruments for musicians, did so because there was something in that player that inspired or appealed to them. It's the same as with any artist except that for musicians the tools of their trade are unaffordable, so they need the benefactors. The reward for the patron is that the performances take on an even greater meaning and become an experience that a painting or sculpture can't give. Music is a series of emotional reactions in time.

Wulfson, of course, has the best and last word:

Immortality is not to be judged, but it is important to make the definition of what is the meaning of the question. If it is the ability to live forever, eternal life, and the quality of deserving to be remembered forever? In this respect, we could talk about professional immortality, when your great colleagues and friends would judge or if we talk about being human, it is more deep, because then it is a question of survival. We should look in the past. Today and in the future. In this respect we should see in the past. By my judgement, the great composers, Bach, Mozart, Beethoven, would not be in question. If we would question this immortality we would need to see a specialist to help us! The best of immortality is our reaction in the fields of art, paintings, sculpture, the question is not only our judgement about immortality, but also about today to compare. To plan immortality for the future is a bit megalomaniac. This kind of planning of immortality is a big trap because of a mixture of corruption of power position in the field and mediocrity… It is a Salieri moment. The question is where to find the Mozart?

To be subjective and serious, immortality is about survival, how to survive, philosophically speaking. It drives us in the direction of maximum mobilization to use our energy to see, smell, observe and use all the perceptions we could develop and should develop in the field of music because we are musicians. When I mention audio, ears, then we deal with matters of my personality as teacher and pedagogue for the most amazing soloists of an amazing capacity. And as an expert and dealer of the most important and amazing rare string instruments. Without these composers it would be difficult to understand timelessness. When we mention Bach, Mozart, Beethoven, and all other geniuses, craftsmen and creators are on the same level, Stradivari, del Gesù, Amati – those are examples of a smaller part of our connections to immortality in the past. If and when we see today's world it makes me, personally, feel, at least that from immortality, from an aesthetic of the highest possible human achievement, is to be like human gods as Vasari said in his book about the artists of the renaissance are half god half human. Stradivari who made the phenomenal quantity of genius instruments, born in 1644, started his craftsmanship from Amati period to the Golden Period, and he created divine instruments which are used today. We cannot imagine that he could think or feel that the virtuoso could play Prokofiev 2, Paganini, Brahms, Shostakovich 1, Bartok – it is the creator of the instrument that is very much in advance before the creator of the music.

Time is very funny. Maybe I am too emotional, to cry about time, because if someone can make such an instrument to be appreciated in a good acoustic, it is unbelievably immortal and something metaphysical. I do not mean time in the literal sense, that this phenomenal music from one period comes to those instruments through the abilities and responsibilities of the living musicians in yet another period of time. If we should create the college of connoisseurs of having the expertise to make a new collection that could be distributed in a way of truth and seriousness, it would be marvellous for business and cultural achievement. That is the goal. Humanity is better served.

Indeed, humanity has benefited over 300 years from the craftsmanship and art that is the rare string instrument. While other instruments are collectibles that allow similar investment returns and even identification with a celebrity, think Jimi Hendrix's guitar or the piano once owned by Mozart, the string instrument is more closely connected to the genius of the maker, not only the brilliance of the player. Immortality is not only about living forever. It also allows time travel, to be present at the moment the instrument is crafted and made, and, like the movie *The Red Violin* shows, to witness its journey through the centuries, coddled by composers and caressed by the greatest virtuosi in the name of aristocracy and art, until at last, to the present day, it is held beneath the chin, bow raised in motion, and a glorious, timeless, immortal sound is heard now and forever. That is what makes the investment worthy and the investor rewarded: With some music, even more money, and, yes, immortality.

CPSIA information can be obtained
at www.ICGtesting.com
Printed in the USA
BVHW031820210421
605556BV00001B/31